Fine Things for Plain Occasions

Fine Things for Plain Occasions

Patterns Inspired by Vintage Etiquette Guides

Hunter Hammersen

PANTSVILLE
PRESS

Text © 2015, Hunter Hammersen

Charts © 2015, Hunter Hammersen

Photos © 2015, Zoë Lonergan

Illustrations © 2015, Anna Kuo

Schematics © 2015, Lana Holden

Charts created with Stitchmastery Knitting Chart Editor

ISBN: 978-0-9849982-6-5

First Printing, 2015

Printed in China

Pantsville Press

Cleveland, Ohio

www.pantsvillepress.com

Contents

Introduction

The custom of making persons known to each other is a necessity in good society. It is the basis of an acquaintanceship which may serve for the enjoyment of an hour, or which may ripen into a friendship…An introduction, therefore…is a tacit pledge on the part of the introducer that the persons introduced are fit to come into each others' society.

Rules of Etiquette and Home Culture: Or What to Do and How to Do It
Professor Walter R. Houghton et al., 1884

I was the quiet kid—the one sitting in the corner (occasionally behind the couch or under the table) with her nose in a book trying not to make eye contact with anyone. Books were easy. People were harder.

One of my most-read books was *White Gloves and Party Manners*. It was meant to be a child's first etiquette guide and promised to tell you both "how to act when you are with other people" and "what to do and what to say to make people like you more and to make yourself more at ease at times when you might be nervous and unsure about what you are saying or doing."

That was exactly what I needed. I was quite convinced that if I just committed the book to memory, I would be perfectly poised in any situation. So I did.

It never occurred to me that the advice offered in a book written in the 60s might not work in the 80s. So I dutifully practiced my curtsey and worked out how best to introduce a

1

nun, a senator, and a visiting dignitary. The occasion never arose, but I felt better knowing I was prepared.

It wasn't long before Miss Manners' newspaper columns caught my eye. I still have the copies of her books I rescued from my school's library sale bin. The works of Letitia Baldridge, Amy Vanderbilt, and Emily Post soon joined those of Miss Manners on my shelves.

Somewhere along the way, I also started collecting copies of older, more obscure etiquette guides. They followed me home from used-book stores and second-hand shops. They showed up as Christmas or birthday presents. A friend who knew nothing of my strange proclivities found some at a yard sale and said she wasn't sure why she'd bought them, but somehow they just reminded her of me.

I had long since realized that these books weren't going to tell me how to behave (elbow-length gloves and visiting cards aren't really a part of my life, though I could do with a few more tea parties), but I still found them tremendously comforting. The more I read, the more I realized that *everyone* wonders what to do, what to say, and what to wear (which happens to be the fabulous subtitle of one of my favorite volumes). I am clearly not the only one who occasionally feels a bit uncertain. And if everyone else is busy worrying about what they're supposed to be doing, perhaps they won't have time to pay too much attention to me!

It may seem like a bit of a leap to go from a collection of etiquette books to a book of knitting patterns (though if you've seen my other work, you'll know it's not the oddest place I've found inspiration). But once you

spend a bit of time with them, you'll see it's the most natural thing in the world. These guides were written before books were filled with page after page of color pictures, but their authors still had *very* distinct opinions about what you should be wearing. That means the books are full of marvelous descriptions that you can interpret however you choose.

That's just what I've done here. I've started with delightful quotes from some of my most treasured books and used them to design a whole host of different patterns. Each includes the quote that inspired it (they are far too delicious not to share), and each pattern's name is taken from its quote. (For those of you wondering, the title of the book is also drawn from a particularly amusing line in one of the books.)

And, while the inspiration for the patterns may have come from vintage sources, the pieces themselves are perfectly suited to the modern knitter. There's not a petticoat, corset, or lace handkerchief in the bunch. Instead you'll find socks, shawls, mitts, and hats that will fit perfectly into your wardrobe.

And, should you happen to find yourself at a tea party or called upon to manage a tricky introduction, just remember that we're all making it up as we go. A smile and a bit of conviction will get you through an awful lot. And, if all else fails, dazzle them with your knitting!

By Naughty Design

In a former generation, women hid their ankles, and gave brief glimpses of them only by accident or naughty design. It was then required of a gentleman that he should precede a lady in ascending stairs. To-day, fashion has cleared away all mystery concerning feminine ankles, and a gentleman is permitted to follow the lady as she mounts the stairs.

Etiquette: An Encyclopedia of Good Manners and Social Usage
Gabrielle Rosiere, 1923

I'm not quite sure how much trouble you can get into by showing off your ankles, but if you can arrange it, you have my whole-hearted support. And if you happen to think these fetching socks might help your ankles draw the attention they deserve? Well I support that, too.

SHOWN IN Lush Twist by Uncommon Thread in Tea Smoked. This is a fingering-weight, 80% merino, 10% cashmere, 10% nylon yarn with two plies.

GAUGE AND SIZING 8.5 stitches in 1 inch in stockinette. Fits a foot or leg of 7.25 [8.25, 9, 10.25] inches.

YARDAGE Shown with a 64-stitch cast on which used about 300 yards of yarn. You can probably make any size with 400 yards or less.

NOTES

Use whatever needles give you the right gauge. That's *probably* something between a 0 and a 2, but you must swatch to be sure.

The socks use different Cuff and Heel Charts. Be sure to follow the appropriate charts.

The shaded stitches are used to adjust sizing. On all charts, work the unshaded stitches for the 56 & 70-stitch sizes. Work all stitches for the 64 & 80-stitch sizes.

The stitches surrounded by the red border are repeated to adjust the size of the heel flap. Work them 2 [2, 3, 3] times.

To make the socks mirror each other, start following the Main Chart on row 1 for the first sock and on row 10 for the second sock.

CAST ON Cast on 56 [64, 70, 80] stitches. Place marker and join for working in the round.

CUFF Work the first row of the appropriate Cuff Chart 7 times. Work the second row of the appropriate Cuff Chart once.

LEG Work the Main Chart until sock reaches desired height. To make the socks mirror each other, start following the Main Chart on row 1 for the first sock and on row 10 for the second sock. Stop after completing row 5 or row 14 of the Main Chart.

HEEL FLAP The heel flap is worked over stitches 30–56 [35–64, 37–70, 43–80]. It uses a total of 27 [30, 34, 38] stitches. Be sure to follow the appropriate Heel Chart, depending on which row of the Main Chart you worked last.

Row 1 is a wrong-side row. Row 2 is a right-side row. Work the appropriate Heel Chart 14 [15, 17, 18] times or until heel flap reaches desired length.

HEEL TURN Turn at the end of each row.

Row 1 (WS): Sl1, p15 [16, 18, 20], right-leaning p decrease, p1.
Row 2 (RS): Sl1, k6 [5, 5, 5], left-leaning k decrease, k1.
Row 3 (WS): Sl1, p7 [6, 6, 6], right-leaning p decrease, p1.
Row 4 (RS): Sl1, k8 [7, 7, 7], left-leaning k decrease, k1.
Row 5 (WS): Sl1, p9 [8, 8, 8], right-leaning p decrease, p1.
Row 6 (RS): Sl1, k10 [9, 9, 9], left-leaning k decrease, k1.
Row 7 (WS): Sl1, p11 [10, 10, 10], right-leaning p decrease, p1.
Row 8 (RS): Sl1, k12 [11, 11, 11], left-leaning k decrease, k1.
Row 9 (WS): Sl1, p13 [12, 12, 12], right-leaning p decrease, p1.
Row 10 (RS): Sl1, k14 [13, 13, 13], left-leaning k decrease, k1.

For 64, 70, & 80-stitch sizes, as above plus:
Row 11 (WS): Sl1, p— [14, 14, 14], right-leaning p decrease, p1.
Row 12 (RS): Sl1, k— [15, 15, 15], left-leaning k decrease, k1.

For 70 & 80-stitch sizes, as above plus:
Row 13 (WS): Sl1, p— [—, 16, 16], right-leaning p decrease, p1.
Row 14 (RS): Sl1, k— [—, 17, 17], left-leaning k decrease, k1.

For 80-stitch size, as above plus:
Row 15 (WS): Sl1, p— [—, —, 18], right-leaning p decrease, p1.
Row 16 (RS): Sl1, k— [—, —, 19], left-leaning k decrease, k1.

17 [18, 20, 22] stitches remain.

GUSSET AND FOOT

SETUP ROUND Pick up and knit stitches along the side of the heel flap, place first marker. Work across the top of the foot following the next row of the Main Chart (for the foot, you will always work 4 [4, 5, 5] full repeats of the Main Chart and 1 [2, 1, 2] additional purl stitches), place second marker. Pick up and knit stitches along the other side of the heel flap, k8 [9, 10, 11]. The round now begins in the middle of the bottom of the foot.

DECREASE ROUND Knit until 3 stitches remain before first marker, right-leaning k decrease, k1. Work across the top of the foot following the next row of the Main Chart. K1, left-leaning k decrease, knit to end of round. 2 stitches decreased.

NON-DECREASE ROUND Knit to first marker. Work across the top of the foot following the next row of the Main Chart. Knit to end of round.

Alternate decrease and non-decrease rounds until 58 [68, 72, 84] stitches remain. Repeat the non-decrease round until sock measures 1.75 [2, 2.25, 2.75] inches shorter than desired length. Stop after completing row 5 or 14 of the Main Chart. Repeat row 5 or 14 of the Main Chart as needed to adjust length.

TOE

DECREASE ROUND Knit until 3 stitches remain before first marker, right-leaning k decrease, k1. P1 [2, 1, 2], left-leaning twisted k decrease, follow ribbing as established by row 5 or 14 of the Main Chart until 3 [4, 3, 4] stitches remain before second marker, right-leaning twisted k decrease, p1 [2, 1, 2]. K1, left-leaning k decrease, knit to end of round. 4 stitches decreased.

NON-DECREASE ROUND Knit to first marker. Follow ribbing as established by row 5 or 14 of the Main Chart to second marker. Knit to end of round.

Work these 2 rounds 4 [6, 7, 10] times, 42 [44, 44, 44] stitches remain. Work the decrease round 5 more times, 22 [24, 24, 24] stitches remain. Knit to first marker. Remove markers. Graft toes. Weave in ends.

LEFT CUFF CHART

RIGHT CUFF CHART

MAIN CHART

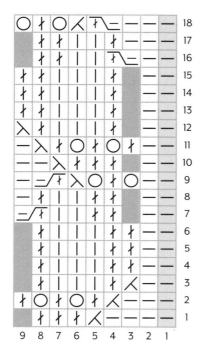

⎢	RS: Knit WS: Purl
⸸	RS: Knit through the back loop WS: Purl through the back loop
—	RS: Purl WS: Knit
◯	Yarn over
→	Slip as if to purl
⟋	Right-leaning twisted knit decrease
⟍	Left-leaning twisted knit decrease
—⟋⸸	1 x 1 Cable right twisted over purl
⸸⟍—	1 x 1 Cable left twisted over purl
▢	Work these stitches 2 [2, 3, 3] times
(light gray)	Work for 64 & 80-stitch size
(dark gray)	No stitch

HEEL CHART (IF YOU STOPPED AFTER ROW 5)

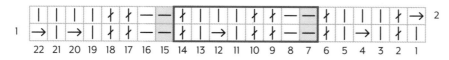

HEEL CHART (IF YOU STOPPED AFTER ROW 14)

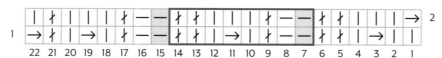

Stitch Guide

RIGHT-LEANING KNIT DECREASE Knit 2 together.

RIGHT-LEANING TWISTED KNIT DECREASE Slip 1 as if to purl. Remount the next stitch so it is rotated 180 degrees (one half turn) clockwise. Return the slipped stitch to the left needle. Knit 2 together.

RIGHT-LEANING PURL DECREASE Purl 2 together.

LEFT-LEANING KNIT DECREASE Slip 1 knitwise. Slip another 1 knitwise. Return slipped stitches to the left needle. Insert the right needle from the right to the left into the back loops of both stitches. Knit both together.

LEFT-LEANING TWISTED KNIT DECREASE Insert the right needle from the right to the left into the back loops of 2 stitches. Knit both together.

1 X 1 CABLE RIGHT TWIST OVER PURL Slip 1 to cable needle, hold in back, knit 1 through the back loop, purl 1 from cable needle.

1 X 1 CABLE LEFT TWIST OVER PURL Slip 1 to cable needle, hold in front, purl 1, knit 1 through the back loop from cable needle.

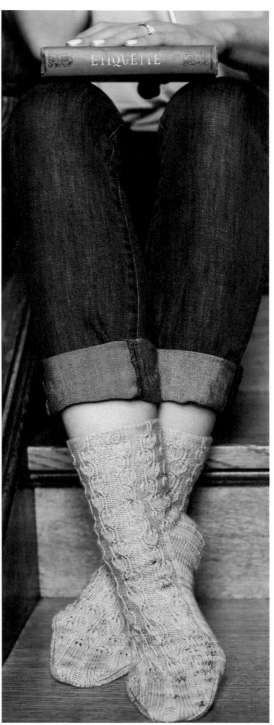

A Lady is Known

That "a lady is known by her gloves and her boots" has passed into a proverb, so any carelessness or untidiness in these important details will place her "beyond the pale." Whether she has a maid or is her own tirewoman, no neglect in the care of the small belongings of dress is tolerated.

Correct Social Usage:
A Course of Instruction in Good Form, Style and Deportment
The New York Society of Self-Culture, 1907

I'm not going to judge your boots (given the state of my own, I have no room to talk). But I do think there's something to be said for a charming pair of gloves.

These will do quite nicely. The richly textured cuff looks much harder than it is, and the plain stockinette hand is both quick to work and supremely comfortable. You'll have a pair (or maybe several) finished in no time.

SHOWN IN Carnal by Vice in Concrete. This is a fingering-weight, 70% merino, 20% cashmere, 10% silk yarn with three plies.

GAUGE AND SIZING 7 stitches in 1 inch in stockinette. Fits a wrist of 5.75 [6.25, 7, 7.5] inches.

YARDAGE Shown with a 36-stitch cast on which used about 100 yards of yarn. You can probably make any size with 175 yards or less.

NOTES

Use whatever needles give you the right gauge. That's *probably* something between a 1 and a 3, but you must swatch to be sure.

The left and right mitts use different instructions for the thumb gusset. Be sure to follow the appropriate instructions

CAST ON Cast on 32 [36, 40, 44] stitches. Place marker and join for working in the round.

CUFF Work the Cuff Chart once.

THUMB OVERVIEW To make the thumb, you will gradually create 12 [12, 14, 14] extra stitches as described below.

LEFT THUMB GUSSET Place a new marker after stitch 4 [4, 5, 5]. Knit to marker, slip marker, yarn over, knit to end of round. Work this round 12 [12, 14, 14] times. 12 [12, 14, 14] stitches increased.

RIGHT THUMB GUSSET Place a new marker 4 [4, 5, 5] stitches before the end of the round. Knit to marker, yarn over, slip marker, knit to end of round. Work this round 12 [12, 14, 14] times. 12 [12, 14, 14] stitches increased.

HAND, PART 1 Knit all stitches for 8 [8, 10, 10] rounds or until cuff reaches the middle of your palm.

HAND, PART 2 Locate and set aside the 12 [12, 14, 14] stitches created for the thumb (these will be the 12 [12, 14, 14] stitches after the new marker for the left cuff or the 12 [12, 14, 14] stitches before the new marker for the right cuff) on a spare needle or length of scrap yarn. Remove the new marker used to create the thumb stitches. Knit all stitches for 6 [6, 8, 8] rounds or until cuff reaches base of your fingers. Purl all stitches for 5 rounds. Bind off loosely.

THUMB Divide the 12 [12, 14, 14] stitches set aside for the thumb across two needles. Pick up 3 stitches to bridge the gap between the first and last of the set-aside thumb stitches. Knit all stitches for 6 [6, 8, 8] rounds. Purl all stitches for 5 rounds. Bind off loosely.

FINISHING Weave in ends. Block if desired.

CUFF CHART

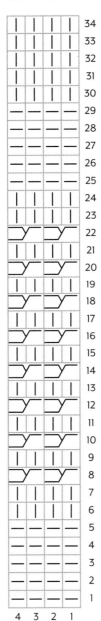

	Knit
—	Purl
⅄	Gather 2 left

STITCH GUIDE

GATHER 2 LEFT Knit 2 together but leave the stitches on the left-hand needle. Knit together into the back loops of the same 2 stitches and this time take them off the left-hand needle as usual.

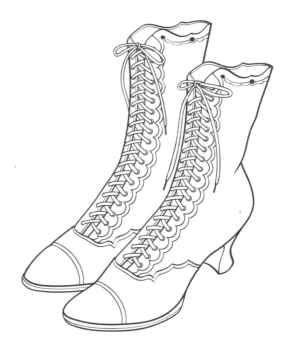

Essential to Perfection

The fit of the stocking is almost as essential to the perfection of the foot as that of the boot or the shoe itself. It should be large enough to allow freedom to the toes, and not so large as to wrinkle on the foot. In a well-fitting stocking the foot can be more accurately measured than otherwise, and the comfort of the foot is sadly impeded by an ill-fitting one.

Social Life or The Manners and Customs of Polite Society
Maud C Cooke, 1896

A custom fit is one of the many points in favor of hand-knit socks. With five sizes and stretchy panels of one-by-one ribbing on the sides, these socks are sure to fit beautifully. I can't quite promise they'll leave you with perfect feet, but I'm sure they'll be a good start.

SHOWN IN Finch by Quince & Co in Iceland. This is a fingering-weight, 100% wool yarn with four plies.

GAUGE AND SIZING 8.5 stitches in 1 inch in stockinette. Fits a foot or leg of 6.75 [7.57, 8.75, 9.75, 10.75] inches.

YARDAGE Shown with a 64-stitch cast on which used about 300 yards of yarn. You can probably make any size with 400 yards or less.

NOTES

Use whatever needles give you the right gauge. That's *probably* something between a 0 and a 2, but you must swatch to be sure.

The stitches surrounded by the red border are repeated to adjust the size of the leg. Work them 0 [1, 2, 3, 4] times.

The stitches surrounded by the purple border are repeated to adjust the size of the heel flap. Work them 11 [13, 15, 17, 19] times.

To make the socks mirror each other, start following the Main Chart on row 1 for the first sock and on row 7 for the second sock.

CAST ON Cast on 48 [56, 64, 72, 80] stitches. Place marker and join for working in the round.

CUFF Work the first row of the Cuff Chart 6 times. Work rows 2 and 3 of the Cuff Chart once. Row 2 of the Cuff Chart increases the stitch count by 4, new stitch count 52 [60, 68, 76, 84].

LEG Work the Main Chart until sock reaches desired height. To make the socks mirror each other, start following the Main Chart on row 1 for the first sock and on row 7 for the second sock. Stop after completing row 6 or row 12 of the Main Chart.

HEEL FLAP The heel flap is worked over stitches 28–52 [32–60, 36–68, 40–76, 44–84]. It uses a total of 25 [29, 33, 37, 41] stitches.

Row 1 is a wrong-side row. Row 2 is a right-side row. Work the Heel Chart 13 [15, 17, 19, 21] times or until heel flap reaches desired length.

HEEL TURN Turn at the end of each row.

Row 1 (WS): Sl1, p13 [15, 17, 19, 21], right-leaning p decrease, p1.
Row 2 (RS): Sl1, k4 [4, 4, 4, 4], left-leaning k decrease, k1.
Row 3 (WS): Sl1, p5 [5, 5, 5, 5], right-leaning p decrease, p1.
Row 4 (RS): Sl1, k6 [6, 6, 6, 6], left-leaning k decrease, k1.
Row 5 (WS): Sl1, p7 [7, 7, 7, 7], right-leaning p decrease, p1.
Row 6 (RS): Sl1, k8 [8, 8, 8, 8], left-leaning k decrease, k1.
Row 7 (WS): Sl1, p9 [9, 9, 9, 9], right-leaning p decrease, p1.
Row 8 (RS): Sl1, k10 [10, 10, 10, 10], left-leaning k decrease, k1.
Row 9 (WS): Sl1, p11 [11, 11, 11, 11], right-leaning p decrease, p1.
Row 10 (RS): Sl1, k12 [12, 12, 12, 12], left-leaning k decrease, k1.

For 56, 64, 72, & 80-stitch sizes, as above plus:
Row 11 (WS): Sl1, p— [13, 13, 13, 13], right-leaning p decrease, p1.
Row 12 (RS): Sl1, k— [14, 14, 14, 14], left-leaning k decrease, k1.

For 64, 72, & 80-stitch sizes, as above plus:
Row 13 (WS): Sl1, p— [—, 15, 15, 15], right-leaning p decrease, p1.
Row 14 (RS): Sl1, k— [—, 16, 16, 16], left-leaning k decrease, k1.

For 72 & 80-stitch sizes, as above plus:
Row 15 (WS): Sl1, p— [—, —, 17, 17], right-leaning p decrease, p1.
Row 16 (RS): Sl1, k— [—, —, 18, 18], left-leaning k decrease, k1.

For 80-stitch size, as above plus:
Row 17 (WS): Sl1, p— [—, —, 19], right-leaning p decrease, p1.
Row 18 (RS): Sl1, k— [—, —, 20], left-leaning k decrease, k1.

15 [17, 19, 21, 23] stitches remain.

GUSSET AND FOOT

SETUP ROUND Pick up and knit stitches along the side of the heel flap, place first marker. Work across the top of the foot following the next row of the Main Chart (for the foot, you will always work 1 full repeat of the Main Chart and 1 additional purl stitch), place second marker. Pick up and knit stitches along the other side of the heel flap, k8 [9, 10, 11, 12]. The round now begins in the middle of the bottom of the foot.

DECREASE ROUND Knit until 3 stitches remain before first marker, right-leaning k decrease, k1. Work across the top of the foot following the next row of the Main Chart. K1, left-leaning k decrease, knit to end of round. 2 stitches decreased.

NON-DECREASE ROUND Knit to first marker. Work across the top of the foot following the next row of the Main Chart. Knit to end of round.

Alternate decrease and non-decrease rounds until 54 [62, 70, 78, 86] stitches remain. Repeat the non-decrease round until sock measures 1.5 [1.75, 2, 2.25, 2.5] inches shorter than desired length. Stop after completing row 6 or row 12 of the Main Chart. Repeat row 3 of the Cuff Chart as needed to adjust length.

TOE

DECREASE ROUND Knit until 3 stitches remain before first marker, right-leaning k decrease, k1. P1, left-leaning twisted k decrease, follow ribbing as established by row 3 of the Cuff Chart until 3 stitches remain before second marker, right-leaning twisted k decrease, p1. K1, left-leaning k decrease, knit to end of round. 4 stitches decreased.

NON-DECREASE ROUND Knit to first marker. Follow ribbing as established by row 3 of the Cuff Chart to second marker. Knit to end of round.

Work these 2 rounds 2 [4, 6, 8, 10] times, 46 stitches remain. Work the decrease round 6 more times, 22 stitches remain. Knit to first marker. Remove markers. Graft toes. Weave in ends.

CUFF CHART

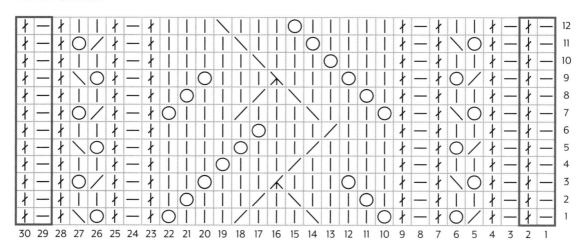

MAIN CHART

HEEL CHART

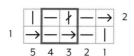

	RS: Knit WS: Purl
⊬	Knit through the back loop
—	RS: Purl WS: Knit
→	Slip as if to purl
○	Yarn over
/	Right-leaning knit decrease
\	Left-leaning knit decrease
⋏	Right-leaning double knit decrease
⋌	Left-leaning double knit decrease
☐	Work these stiches 0 [1, 2, 3, 4] times
☐	Work these stitches 11 [13, 15, 17, 19] times
▨	No stitch

24

STITCH GUIDE

RIGHT-LEANING KNIT DECREASE Knit 2 together.

RIGHT-LEANING TWISTED KNIT DECREASE Slip 1 as if to purl. Remount the next stitch so it is rotated 180 degrees (one half turn) clockwise. Return the slipped stitch to the left needle. Knit 2 together.

RIGHT-LEANING PURL DECREASE Purl 2 together.

LEFT-LEANING KNIT DECREASE Slip 1 knitwise. Slip another 1 knitwise. Return slipped stitches to the left needle. Insert the right needle from the right to the left into the back loops of both stitches. Knit both together.

LEFT-LEANING TWISTED KNIT DECREASE Insert the right needle from the right to the left into the back loops of 2 stitches. Knit both together.

RIGHT-LEANING DOUBLE KNIT DECREASE Slip 1 knitwise. Slip another 1 knitwise. Return slipped stitches to the left needle. Insert the right needle from the right to the left into the back loops of both stitches. Knit both together. Put the resulting stitch back on the left needle. Pass the second stitch on the left needle over the first. Slip the first stitch back to the right needle.

LEFT-LEANING DOUBLE KNIT DECREASE Slip 1 knitwise. Knit 2 together. Pass slipped stitch over.

Just Which is in Vogue

When one is uncertain about just which is in vogue a happy medium can be reached by buying dresses that do not disclose too much epidermis. Wear shoulder covering enough to exclude you from the old story of the man who when being asked by his wife what the women wore at a banquet he had attended without her, said dryly, "From where I was sitting, I couldn't tell."

The New Etiquette: The Modern Code of Social Behavior
Margery Wilson, 1937

I'm fairly certain your opinions (rather than those of your dinner companions) should dictate what you wear. But, if you happen to feel like putting something around your shoulders, this shawl would be a lovely choice. The curved edge makes it easy to wear, and the intricate lace is sure to catch everyone's eye.

SHOWN IN Lust by Alchemy: Yarns of Transformation in Amethyst. This is a sport-weight, 70% wool, 30% silk yarn with twelve very tiny plies.

GAUGE AND SIZING 28 stitches in 4 inches in pattern as shown in Lower Chart. The blocked shawl measures about 46 [55, 64] inches across at the top edge.

YARDAGE Shown with a 411-stitch cast on which used about 650 yards of yarn. You can probably make any size with 800 yards or less.

NOTES

Use whatever needles give you the right gauge. That's *probably* something between a 3 and a 5, but you must swatch to be sure.

The stitches surrounded by the red border are repeated to adjust the size of the shawl. Work them 11 [13, 15] times when working the Lower Chart and Transition Chart and 9 [11, 13] times when working the Upper Chart.

CAST ON Using a very stretchy cast on (the Chinese Waitress cast on is a good choice, and there are several marvelous videos on YouTube), cast on 351 [411, 471] stitches.

LOWER EDGING Odd rows are right-side rows. Even rows are wrong-side rows. Work the Lower Chart 4 times.

TRANSITION Odd rows are right-side rows. Even rows are wrong-side rows. Work the Transition Chart 1 time.

BODY You will now shape the body by working a section of short rows. This will be much easier if you mark off the center stitch of the piece before you start (it will save you a lot of counting). The center stitch is the 176th [206th, 236th] stitch.

Odd rows are right-side rows. Even rows are wrong-side rows.

Row 1 (RS): Sl1, k to center stitch, k center stitch, k7, turn.
Row 2 (WS): Sl1, p to center stitch, p center stitch, p7, turn.
Row 3 (RS): Sl1, k to previous turning point, left-leaning k decrease, k3, turn.
Row 4 (WS): Sl1, p to previous turning point, right-leaning p decrease, p3, turn.

Work rows 3 and 4 30 times. 60 stitches decreased, 291 [351, 411] stitches remaining.

Row 5 (RS): Sl1, knit to end.

UPPER EDGING Odd rows are wrong-side rows. Even rows are right-side rows. Work the Upper Chart 1 time.

FINISHING Bind off loosely, weave in ends. Block as described.

BLOCKING Start by pinning out the upper edge straight. I recommend placing pins in the holes made by the double yarn overs to emphasize them. The upper edge should be about 46 [55, 64] inches long. Then pin out the left and right sides straight. The sides should be about 12 inches long. Now evenly pin out the bottom edge, being sure to emphasize the curve created by the short rows.

STITCH GUIDE

RIGHT-LEANING PURL DECREASE Purl 2 together.

LEFT-LEANING KNIT DECREASE Slip 1 knitwise. Slip another 1 knitwise. Return slipped stitches to the left needle. Insert the right needle from the right to the left into the back loops of both stitches. Knit both together.

CENTERED QUADRUPLE DECREASE OVERVIEW These decreases start by reorienting the first 3 stitches of the decrease in a particular way, then working a decrease with the next 2 stitches, then passing the 3 stitches you reoriented, as a group, back over the stitch you just made. The specifics are given below for right-side and wrong-side versions, but if you hold this overview idea in mind, it helps.

CENTERED QUADRUPLE KNIT DECREASE Slip 3 together at the same time as if to knit. Knit 2 together. Pass the 3 slipped stitches, together as a set, over the stitch you just made.

CENTERED QUADRUPLE PURL DECREASE Slip 1 knitwise 3 times. Return these 3 stitches to the left needle in their new orientation. Swing your right needle around behind the fabric and insert it into these 3 stitches, from left to right, and slip them to your right needle. Slip 1 knitwise. Slip another 1 knitwise. Return just these 2 slipped stitches to the left needle. Purl 2 together through the back loops. Pass the 3 slipped stitches, together as a set, over the stitch you just made.

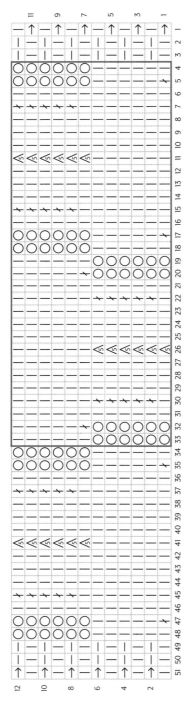

	RS: Knit
	WS: Purl

	RS: Knit through the back loop
	WS: Purl through the back loop

	RS: Purl
	WS: Knit

| ↑ | Slip as if to purl |

| ○ | Yarn over |

	RS: Centered quadruple knit decrease
	WS: Centered quadruple purl decrease

| | Work these stitches as described in the pattern |

Transition Chart

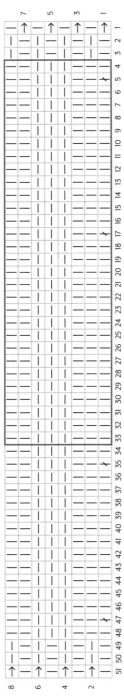

Upper Chart

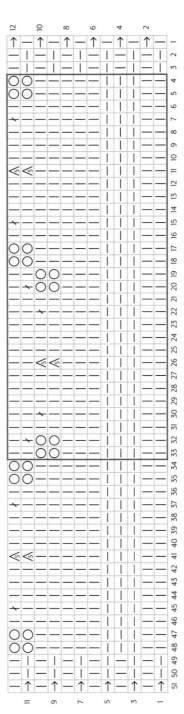

General Country Sports

For cycling and general country sports, men wear knickerbocker suits of tweed, Norfolk or short jackets, heavy ribbed golf stockings, stout russet laced shoes, and cloth caps or soft felt Homburg hats.

Etiquette for All Occasions
Mrs. Burton Kingsland, 1901

I'm not all that sure I do much that falls under the heading of general country sports. But I am a big fan of excellent socks. And these (sized for both ladies and gentlemen, because everyone needs a good sock) fit the bill quite nicely. They're thick enough to be comfy on a long hike (or curled up at home in front of the fire, I won't tell), and the cables are delightfully dramatic.

SHOWN IN Ghillie Sport by Bare Naked Wools in Cream. This is a sport-weight, 100% cheviot yarn with four plies.

GAUGE AND SIZING 7.5 stitches in 1 inch in stockinette. Fits a foot or leg of 7.25 [8.5, 9.75, 10.75, 12] inches.

YARDAGE Shown with a 66-stitch cast on which used about 325 yards of yarn. You can probably make any size with 425 yards or less.

NOTES

Use whatever needles give you the right gauge. That's *probably* something between a 1 and a 3, but you must swatch to be sure.

The stitches surrounded by the red border are repeated to adjust the size of the sock. Work them 1 [2, 3, 4, 5] times.

CAST ON Cast on 50 [58, 66, 74, 82] stitches. Place marker and join for working in the round.

LEG Work the Main Chart until sock reaches desired height. Stop after completing row 4 or 8 of the Main Chart.

HEEL FLAP The heel flap is worked over stitches 27–50 [31–58, 35–66, 39–74, 43–82]. It uses a total of 24 [28, 32, 36, 40] stitches.

Row 1 is a wrong-side row. Row 2 is a right-side row. Work the Heel Chart 6 [7, 8, 9, 10] times or until heel flap reaches desired length.

HEEL TURN Turn at the end of each row.

Row 1 (WS): Sl1, p14 [16, 18, 20, 22], right-leaning p decrease, p1.
Row 2 (RS): Sl1, k7 [7, 7, 7, 7], left-leaning k decrease, k1.
Row 3 (WS): Sl1, p8 [8, 8, 8, 8], right-leaning p decrease, p1.
Row 4 (RS): Sl1, k9 [9, 9, 9, 9], left-leaning k decrease, k1.
Row 5 (WS): Sl1, p10 [10, 10, 10, 10], right-leaning p decrease, p1.
Row 6 (RS): Sl1, k11 [11, 11, 11, 11], left-leaning k decrease, k1.
Row 7 (WS): Sl1, p12 [12, 12, 12, 12], right-leaning p decrease, p1.
Row 8 (RS): Sl1, k13 [13, 13, 13, 13], left-leaning k decrease, k1.

For 58, 66, 74, & 82-stitch sizes as above plus:
Row 9 (WS): Sl1, p— [14, 14, 14, 14], right-leaning p decrease, p1.
Row 10 (RS): Sl1, k— [15, 15, 15, 15], left-leaning k decrease, k1.

For 66, 74, & 82-stitch sizes as above plus:
Row 11 (WS): Sl1, p— [—, 16, 16, 16], right-leaning p decrease, p1.
Row 12 (RS): Sl1, k— [—, 17, 17, 17], left-leaning k decrease, k1.

For 74 & 82-stitch sizes as above plus:
Row 13 (WS): Sl1, p— [—, —, 18, 18], right-leaning p decrease, p1.
Row 14 (RS): Sl1, k— [—, —, 19, 19], left-leaning k decrease, k1.

For 82-stitch size, as above plus:
Row 15 (WS): Sl1, p— [—, —, –, 20], right-leaning p decrease, p1.
Row 16 (RS): Sl1, k— [—, —, –, 21], left-leaning k decrease, k1.

16 [18, 20, 22, 24] stitches remain.

GUSSET AND FOOT

SETUP ROUND Pick up and knit stitches along the side of the heel flap, place first marker. Work across the top of the foot following the next row of the Main Chart (for the foot, you will always work 1 full repeat of the Main Chart and 1 additional knit stitch), place second marker. Pick up and knit stitches along the other side of the heel

flap, k8 [9, 10, 11, 12]. The round now begins in the middle of the bottom of the foot.

DECREASE ROUND Knit until 3 stitches remain before first marker, right-leaning k decrease, p1. Work across the top of the foot following the next row of the Main Chart. P1, left-leaning k decrease, knit to end of round. 2 stitches decreased.

NON-DECREASE ROUND Knit until 1 stitch remains before first marker, p1. Work across the top of the foot following the next row of the Main Chart. P1, knit to end of round.

Alternate decrease and non-decrease rounds until 52 [60, 68, 76, 84] stitches remain. Repeat the non-decrease round until sock measures 1.75 [2.25, 2.75, 3.25, 3.75] inches shorter than desired length. Stop after completing row 4 or row 8 of the Main Chart. Repeat row 1 of the Main Chart as needed to adjust length.

TOE

DECREASE ROUND Knit until 3 stitches remain before first marker, right-leaning k decrease, p1. K1, p1, left-leaning k decrease, follow ribbing as established by row 1 of the Main Chart until 4 stitches remain before second marker, right-leaning k decrease, p1, k1. P1, left-leaning k decrease, knit to end of round. 4 stitches decreased.

NON-DECREASE ROUND Knit until 1 stitch remains before first marker, p1. Follow ribbing as established by row 1 of the Main Chart to second marker. P1, knit to end of round.

Work these 2 rounds 2 [4, 6, 8, 10] times, 44 stitches remain. Work the decrease round 6 more times, 20 stitches remain. Knit to first marker. Remove markers. Graft toes. Weave in ends.

Main Chart

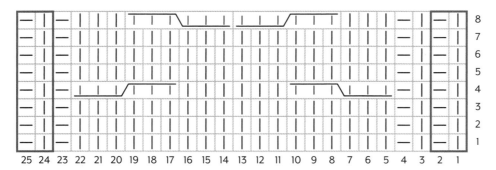

Heel Chart

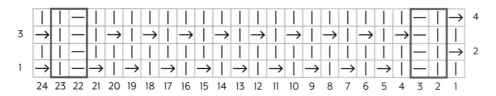

	RS: Knit
	WS: Purl

	RS: Purl
	WS: Knit

→ Slip as if to purl

| | | | / | | | | 3 x 3 Cable right

| | | \ | | | | 3 x 3 Cable left

☐ Work these stitches 1 [2, 3, 4, 5] times

Stitch Guide

RIGHT-LEANING KNIT DECREASE Knit 2 together.

RIGHT-LEANING PURL DECREASE Purl 2 together.

LEFT-LEANING KNIT DECREASE Slip 1 knitwise. Slip another 1 knitwise. Return slipped stitches to the left needle. Insert the right needle from the right to the left into the back loops of both stitches. Knit both together.

3 X 3 CABLE RIGHT Slip 3 to cable needle, hold in back, knit 3, knit 3 from cable needle.

3 X 3 CABLE LEFT Slip 3 to cable needle, hold in front, knit 3, knit 3 from cable needle.

Suitable for Use

For a week's stay at a gay country house, a young woman will find herself in need of no less than three hats—one a prettily trimmed walking and traveling hat; one…for golfing, boating, or picnicking; and one of more delicate construction suitable for use with light afternoon frocks, for tea parties, etc.

Encyclopaedia of Etiquette: What to Write, What to Wear, What to Do, What to Say, A Book of Manners for Everyday Use
Emily Holt, 1915

Perhaps I can save you a bit of room in your trunk by offering a hat that can be worn several different ways. Both sides of this fabric look lovely, so you can wear it with either side facing out. Try it with the brim folded up for a closer fit or with the brim unfolded for a bit of slouch. With all those options, it might just be enough to see you through a whole week without reinforcements.

SHOWN IN Trinity Worsted by Sweet-Georgia in Silver. This is a worsted-weight, 70% merino, 20% cashmere, 10% silk yarn with four plies.

GAUGE AND SIZING 20 stitches in 4 inches in pattern as shown on Main Chart (the fabric should be quite drapey and crumple easily). Fits a head of 21 [22.5, 23.75, 25] inches.

YARDAGE Shown with a 102-stitch cast on which used about 175 yards of yarn. You can probably make any size with 225 yards or less.

NOTES

Use whatever needles give you the right gauge. That's *probably* something between an 8 and a 10, but you must swatch to be sure. You will also need needles one size smaller than those needed to get gauge.

The hat is reversible, so when you're finished, it's up to you to decide which side is the inside. But, in the instructions, the side with the floats will be called the inside. That means the first two pictures show the inside, and the last two show the outside, as the pattern is written.

CAST ON Cast on 96 [102, 108, 114] stitches. Place marker and join for working in the round.

BRIM Using needles one size smaller than those needed to get gauge, work row 1 of the Main Chart until hat measures 2 inches tall (or until you reach your desired depth of brim if you have strong feelings about hat brims).

BODY To make the ribbing draw together nicely, you need to pay a bit of extra attention when you're working row 2 of the Main Chart. You want your floats (the strands of yarn created when you slip stitches) to be drawn rather tightly. This is the opposite of what you often want when working floats. To help achieve this, I recommend pushing the three stitches to be slipped close to each other and slipping all three together at one time. I also recommend giving the yarn a little extra tug when you work stitch 5 of row 2 of the Main Chart. This will help shorten the float and bring stitches 1 and 5 closer to each other.

Using needles needed to get gauge, work the Main Chart until hat reaches desired height before the decreases. Stop after completing row 2 of the Main Chart.

The decreases happen very quickly (in just eight rounds). You won't get any extra height from them. Be sure the hat is as tall as you'd like it to be before you begin working the decreases. If you know for sure you only plan to wear it with the brim folded or unfolded, be sure you're measuring it that way. Shown here with 9 inches total length before decrease (2 for the brim, 7 for the body), which makes a close-fitting hat with the brim folded and a slouchy hat with it unfolded.

DECREASES Work the Decrease Chart once. 16 [17, 18, 19] stitches remain. Work 8 [8, 9, 9] left-leaning k decreases. 8 [9, 9, 10] stitches remain.

FINISHING Draw the yarn through remaining stitches. Weave in ends (be sure to be neat, because both sides may show). Block if desired.

MAIN CHART

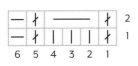

−	⅄	−	−	−	⅄	2
−	⅄	|	|	|	⅄	1

6 5 4 3 2 1

DECREASE CHART

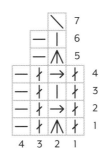

		＼		7
	−	|		6
	−	∧		5
−	⅄	→	⅄	4
−	⅄	|	⅄	3
−	⅄	→	⅄	2
−	⅄	∧	⅄	1

4 3 2 1

|	Knit
⅄	Knit through the back loop
−	Purl
→	Slip as if to purl
———	Slip 3
＼	Left-leaning knit decrease
∧	Centered double knit decrease

STITCH GUIDE

SLIP 3 Slip 3 stitches as if to purl with the yarn held to the inside of the hat.

LEFT-LEANING KNIT DECREASE Slip 1 knitwise. Slip another 1 knitwise. Return slipped stitches to the left needle. Insert the right needle from the right to the left into the back loops of both stitches. Knit both together.

CENTERED DOUBLE KNIT DECREASE Slip 2 together at the same time as if to knit 2 together. Knit 1. Pass the slipped stitches over.

Knowledge of What was Sensible

If [a] woman were going to walk for pleasure or health, she would show her knowledge of what was sensible and suitable by putting on thick stockings, ribbed silk or silk and wool, and thick-soled shoes with low heels.

Vogue's Book of Etiquette: Present-day Customs of Social Intercourse with the Rules for their Correct Observance
The Editors of Vogue, 1925

I don't mind being sensible and suitable—at least not most of the time. But I'm not convinced that those virtues should be reserved just for women. To that end, I offer a sock that is eminently suitable for (and sized for) both ladies and gentlemen.

SHOWN IN Staccato by Shibui in Caffeine. This is a fingering-weight, 70% superwash merino, 30% silk yarn with two plies.

GAUGE AND SIZING 8.5 stitches in 1 inch in stockinette. Fits a foot or leg of 7.25 [8.25, 9, 10.25, 10.75] inches.

YARDAGE Shown with a 64-stitch cast on which used about 300 yards of yarn. You can probably make any size with 450 yards or less.

NOTES

Use whatever needles give you the right gauge. That's *probably* something between a 0 and a 2, but you must swatch to be sure.

The shaded stitches are used to adjust sizing. On all charts, work the unshaded stitches for the 56, 70, & 84-stitch sizes. Work all stitches for the 64 & 80-stitch sizes.

The stitches surrounded by the red border are repeated to adjust the size of the heel flap. Work them 2 [2, 3, 3, 4] times.

CAST ON Cast on 56 [64, 70, 80, 84] stitches. Place marker and join for working in the round.

CUFF Work the first row of the Main Chart 7 times.

LEG Work the Main Chart until sock reaches desired height. Stop after completing row 2 of the Main Chart.

HEEL FLAP The heel flap is worked over stitches 30–56 [35–64, 37–70, 43–80, 44–84]. It uses a total of 27 [30, 34, 38, 41] stitches.

Row 1 is a wrong-side row. Row 2 is a right-side row. Work the Heel Chart 14 [15, 17, 18, 19] times or until heel flap reaches desired length.

HEEL TURN Turn at the end of each row.

Row 1 (WS): Sl1, p15 [16, 18, 20, 21], right-leaning p decrease, p1.
Row 2 (RS): Sl1, k6 [5, 5, 5, 4], left-leaning k decrease, k1.
Row 3 (WS): Sl1, p7 [6, 6, 6, 5], right-leaning p decrease, p1.
Row 4 (RS): Sl1, k8 [7, 7, 7, 6], left-leaning k decrease, k1.
Row 5 (WS): Sl1, p9 [8, 8, 8, 7], right-leaning p decrease, p1.
Row 6 (RS): Sl1, k10 [9, 9, 9, 8], left-leaning k decrease, k1.
Row 7 (WS): Sl1, p11 [10, 10, 10, 9], right-leaning p decrease, p1.
Row 8 (RS): Sl1, k12 [11, 11, 11, 10], left-leaning k decrease, k1.
Row 9 (WS): Sl1, p13 [12, 12, 12, 11], right-leaning p decrease, p1.
Row 10 (RS): Sl1, k14 [13, 13, 13, 12], left-leaning k decrease, k1.

For 64, 70, 80, & 84-stitch sizes, as above plus:
Row 11 (WS): Sl1, p— [14, 14, 14, 13], right-leaning p decrease, p1.
Row 12 (RS): Sl1, k— [15, 15, 15, 14], left-leaning k decrease, k1.

For 70, 80, & 84-stitch sizes, as above plus:
Row 13 (WS): Sl1, p— [—, 16, 16, 15], right-leaning p decrease, p1.
Row 14 (RS): Sl1, k— [—, 17, 17, 16], left-leaning k decrease, k1.

For 80 & 84-stitch sizes, as above plus:
Row 15 (WS): Sl1, p— [—, —, 18, 17], right-leaning p decrease, p1.
Row 16 (RS): Sl1, k— [—, —, 19, 18], left-leaning k decrease, k1.

For 84-stitch size, as above plus:
Row 17 (WS): Sl1, p— [—, —, 19], right-leaning p decrease, p1.
Row 18 (RS): Sl1, k— [—, —, 20], left-leaning k decrease, k1.

17 [18, 20, 22, 25] stitches remain.

GUSSET AND FOOT

SETUP ROUND Pick up and knit stitches along the side of the heel flap, place first marker. Work across the top of the foot following the first row of the Main Chart (for the foot, you will always work 4 [4, 5, 5, 6] full repeats of the Main Chart and 1 [2, 1, 2, 1] additional purl stitches), place second marker. Pick up and knit stitches along the other side of the heel flap, k8 [9, 10, 11, 12]. The round now begins in the middle of the bottom of the foot.

DECREASE ROUND Knit until 3 stitches remain before first marker, right-leaning k decrease, k1. Work across the top of the foot following the next row of the Main Chart. K1, left-leaning k decrease, knit to end of round. 2 stitches decreased.

NON-DECREASE ROUND Knit to first marker. Work across the top of the foot following the next row of the Main Chart. Knit to end of round.

Alternate decrease and non-decrease rounds until 58 [68, 72, 84, 86] stitches remain. Repeat the non-decrease round until sock measures 1.75 [2, 2.25, 2.75, 2.75] inches shorter than desired length. Stop after completing row 2 of the Main Chart.

TOE

DECREASE ROUND Knit until 3 stitches remain before first marker, right-leaning k decrease, k1. P1 [2, 1, 2, 1], left-leaning twisted k decrease, follow ribbing as established by row 1 of the Main Chart until 3 [4, 3, 4, 3] stitches remain before second marker, right-leaning twisted k decrease, p1 [2, 1, 2, 1]. K1, left-leaning k decrease, knit to end of round. 4 stitches decreased.

NON-DECREASE ROUND Knit to first marker. Follow ribbing as established by row 1 of the Main Chart to second marker. Knit to end of round.

Work these 2 rounds 4 [6, 7, 10, 11] times, 42 [44, 44, 44, 42] stitches remain. Work the decrease round 5 more times, 22 [24, 24, 24, 22] stitches remain. Knit to first marker. Remove markers. Graft toes. Weave in ends.

MAIN CHART

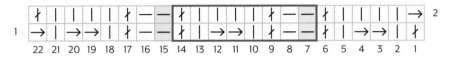

HEEL CHART

RS: Knit WS: Purl

RS: Purl WS: Knit

RS: Knit through the back loop WS: Purl through the back loop

Slip as if to purl

1 x 1 Cable right

1 x 1 Cable left

Work these stitches 2 [2, 3, 3, 4] times

Work for 64 & 80-stitch size

STITCH GUIDE

RIGHT-LEANING KNIT DECREASE Knit 2 together.

RIGHT-LEANING TWISTED KNIT DECREASE Slip 1 as if to purl. Remount the next stitch so it is rotated 180 degrees (one half turn) clockwise. Return the slipped stitch to the left needle. Knit 2 together.

RIGHT-LEANING PURL DECREASE Purl 2 together.

LEFT-LEANING KNIT DECREASE Slip 1 knitwise. Slip another 1 knitwise. Return slipped stitches to the left needle. Insert the right needle from the right to the left into the back loops of both stitches. Knit both together.

LEFT-LEANING TWISTED KNIT DECREASE Insert the right needle from the right to the left into the back loops of 2 stitches. Knit both together.

1 X 1 CABLE RIGHT Slip 1 to cable needle, hold in back, knit 1, knit 1 from cable needle.

1 X 1 CABLE LEFT Slip 1 to cable needle, hold in front, knit 1, knit 1 from cable needle.

54

Treacherous Winds

For the woman with a well-stocked wardrobe few if any additions are required for a transatlantic crossing or for a cruise…She will need a scarf or scarfs to keep treacherous winds from blowing down her neck. If her budget is limited it is an excellent plan to have few frocks and several hats and scarfs which vary the appearance of her outfits.

The New Etiquette: The Modern Code of Social Behavior
Margery Wilson, 1937

Alas, all my transatlantic crossings have been made by airplane. But a selection of hats and scarves to vary the appearance of my outfits still has tremendous appeal (as does the thought of something warm and soft to keep treacherous winds from blowing down my neck). This piece, somewhere between a scarf and a cowl, should do the trick nicely. The arrangement of buttons and the lacy nature of the fabric let you fasten it in a tremendous variety of ways. Experiment and find your favorite.

SHOWN IN Fino by Manos del Uruguay in Rosewater. This is a fingering-weight, 70% merino, 30% silk single-ply yarn.

GAUGE AND SIZING 30 stitches in 4 inches in three by two ribbing. Finished width of 5 [6.25, 7.5] inches at the ends, length is adjustable.

YARDAGE Shown with a 31-stitch cast on which used about 250 yards of yarn. You can probably make any size with 300 yards or less. You'll also want 14 [18, 20] small shank buttons.

NOTES

Use whatever needles give you the right gauge. That's *probably* something between a 1 and a 3, but you must swatch to be sure. You will also need needles 2 sizes larger than those needed to get gauge.

Odd rows are wrong-side rows. Even rows are right-side rows.

The stitches surrounded by the red border are repeated to adjust the size of the piece. Work them 7 [9, 11] times.

The rows surrounded by the gray border are repeated to make the piece wrap comfortably around your neck

Note that your stitch count changes from row to row. After most rows, it will be 39 [49, 59]. After rows 4, 8, and 12, it will be 25 [31, 37].

CAST ON Using needles needed to get gauge, cast on 25 [31, 37] stitches.

FIRST END Work rows 1–4 of the Main Chart until fabric (when stretched to gauge) is square. Stop after completing row 4. Rows 1-4 were worked 16 times in the piece shown, but you should work them as many times as you need to get a square (which will vary depending on your row gauge). Make a note of how many times you worked them. Work row 5 of the Main Chart once.

MIDDLE Switch to needles 2 sizes larger than those used so far. Work rows 6–7 of the Main Chart until the middle part of the scarf is long enough to wrap loosely around your neck with the first end sitting on your collar bones as shown. The middle portion of the piece shown here measures 20 inches.

SECOND END Switch back to smaller needles. Work row 8 of the Main Chart once. Work rows 9–12 of the Main Chart as many times as you worked rows 1–4 of the Main Chart when working the first end.

FINISHING Bind off loosely. Weave in ends. Apply buttons evenly along the top and bottom of the first end as shown in the schematic below. Block, being sure to form the ends into squares.

You can wear it with the ends buttoned at right angles (as in the first picture) or aligned (as in the second picture) or however strikes your fancy.

BUTTON PLACEMENT GUIDE
Starting at the bottom of the schematic and moving up, you see: the cast on edge, one set of buttons, rows 1-4 of the Main Chart repeated as needed, a second set of buttons, row 5 of the Main Chart, and the middle portion of the piece.

MAIN CHART

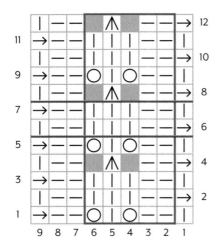

Symbol	Meaning
RS: Knit / WS: Purl	
RS: Purl / WS: Knit	
→	Slip as if to purl
○	Yarn over
∧	Centered double knit decrease
□	Work these stitches 7 [9, 11] times
□	Using larger needles, work these rows until cowl reaches desired length
(shaded)	No stitch

STITCH GUIDE

CENTERED DOUBLE KNIT DECREASE Slip 2 together at the same time as if to knit 2 together. Knit 1. Pass the slipped stitches over.

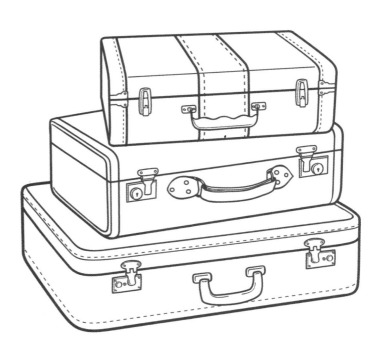

Singularly Disenchanting

If you are not quite certain of the line between neatness and the reverse, be over-scrupulous about your under garments. The edge of a soiled petticoat, or the glimpse of a rent stocking is singularly disenchanting.

The Ladies' Book of Etiquette and Manual of Politeness:
A Complete Hand Book for the Use of the Lady in Polite Society
Florence Hartley, 1860

I don't wish to be contrary, but I actually find these socks quite enchanting. The tiny, twisted cables provide a perfect, structured backdrop for carefully placed drop stitches. As for your other underthings? You're on your own there.

SHOWN IN Shepherd Sock by Lorna's Laces in Buckingham Fountain. This is a fingering-weight, 80% superwash merino, 20% nylon yarn with four plies.

GAUGE AND SIZING 8.5 stitches in 1 inch in stockinette. Fits a foot or leg of 7.25 [8.25, 9.25, 10.25, 11] inches.

YARDAGE Shown with a 64-stitch cast on which used about 300 yards of yarn. You can probably make any size with 425 yards or less.

NOTES

Use whatever needles give you the right gauge. That's *probably* something between a 0 and a 2, but you must swatch to be sure.

The stitches surrounded by the red border are repeated to adjust the size of the sock. Work them 3 [4, 5, 6, 7] times.

The left and right socks use different charts and have different instructions. Be sure to follow the appropriate charts and instructions.

CAST ON Cast on 56 [64, 72, 80, 88] stitches. Place marker and join for working in the round.

CUFF Work the appropriate Cuff Chart 2 times.

LEG Work the appropriate Main Chart until sock reaches desired height. Stop after completing row 12 or row 24 of the Main Chart.

HEEL FLAP The heel flap is worked over stitches 29–56 [33–64, 37–72, 41–80, 45–88]. It uses a total of 28 [32, 36, 40, 44] stitches.

Odd rows are wrong-side rows. Even rows are right-side rows. Work the appropriate Heel Chart 7 [8, 9, 10, 11] times or until heel flap reaches desired length.

HEEL TURN Turn at the end of each row.

Row 1 (WS): Sl1, p16 [18, 20, 22, 24], right-leaning p decrease, p1.
Row 2 (RS): Sl1, k7 [7, 7, 7, 7], left-leaning k decrease, k1.
Row 3 (WS): Sl1, p8 [8, 8, 8, 8], right-leaning p decrease, p1.
Row 4 (RS): Sl1, k9 [9, 9, 9, 9], left-leaning k decrease, k1.
Row 5 (WS): Sl1, p10 [10, 10, 10, 10], right-leaning p decrease, p1.
Row 6 (RS): Sl1, k11 [11, 11, 11, 11], left-leaning k decrease, k1.
Row 7 (WS): Sl1, p12 [12, 12, 12, 12], right-leaning p decrease, p1.
Row 8 (RS): Sl1, k13 [13, 13, 13, 13], left-leaning k decrease, k1.
Row 9 (WS): Sl1, p14 [14, 14, 14, 14], right-leaning p decrease, p1.
Row 10 (RS): Sl1, k15 [15, 15, 15, 15], left-leaning k decrease, k1.

For 64, 72, 80, & 88-stitch sizes, as above plus:
Row 11 (WS): Sl1, p— [16, 16, 16, 16], right-leaning p decrease, p1.
Row 12 (RS): Sl1, k— [17, 17, 17, 17], left-leaning k decrease, k1.

For 72, 80, & 88-stitch sizes, as above plus:
Row 13 (WS): Sl1, p— [—, 18, 18, 18], right-leaning p decrease, p1.
Row 14 (RS): Sl1, k— [—, 19, 19, 19], left-leaning k decrease, k1.

For 80 & 88-stitch sizes, as above plus:
Row 15 (WS): Sl1, p— [—, —, 20, 20], right-leaning p decrease, p1.
Row 16 (RS): Sl1, k— [—, —, 21, 21], left-leaning k decrease, k1.

For 88-stitch size, as above plus:
Row 17 (WS): Sl1, p— [—, —, —, 22], right-leaning p decrease, p1.
Row 18 (RS): Sl1, k— [—, —, —, 23], left-leaning k decrease, k1.

18 [20, 22, 24, 26] stitches remain.

GUSSET AND FOOT

SETUP ROUND Pick up and knit stitches along the side of the heel flap, place first marker. Work across the top of the foot following the next row of the appropriate Main Chart, place second marker. Pick up and knit stitches along the other side of the heel flap, k9 [10, 11, 12, 13]. The round now begins in the middle of the bottom of the foot.

DECREASE ROUND Knit until 3 stitches remain before first marker, right-leaning k decrease, p1. Work across the top of the foot following the next row of the appropriate Main Chart. P1, left-leaning k decrease, knit to end of round. 2 stitches decreased.

NON-DECREASE ROUND Knit until 1 stitch remains before first marker, p1. Work across the top of the foot following the next row of the appropriate Main Chart. P1, knit to end of round.

Alternate decrease and non-decrease rounds until 56 [64, 72, 80, 88] stitches remain. Repeat the non-decrease round until sock measures 1.5 [1.75, 2, 2.25, 2.5] inches shorter than desired length. Stop after completing row 12 or row 24 of the appropriate Main Chart. Repeat row 1 of the appropriate Cuff Chart as needed to adjust length.

TOE

DECREASE ROUND (RIGHT SOCK) Knit until 3 stitches remain before first marker, right-leaning k decrease, p1. P1, knit 1 through the back loop, left-leaning twisted k decrease, follow ribbing as established by row 1 of the appropriate Cuff Chart until 4 stitches remain before second marker, right-leaning k decrease, k1, p1. P1, left-leaning k decrease, knit to end of round. 4 stitches decreased.

DECREASE ROUND (LEFT SOCK) Knit until 3 stitches remain before first marker, right-leaning k decrease, p1. P1, k, left-leaning k decrease, follow ribbing as established by row 1 of the appropriate Cuff Chart until 4 stitches remain before second marker, right-leaning twisted k decrease, knit 1 through the back loop, p1. P1, left-leaning k decrease, knit to end of round. 4 stitches decreased.

NON-DECREASE ROUND Knit until 1 stitch remains before first marker, p1. Follow ribbing as established to second marker. P1, knit to end of round.

Work these 2 rounds 2 [4, 6, 8, 10] times, 48 stitches remain. Work the decrease round 6 more times, 24 stitches remain. Knit to first marker. Remove markers. Graft toes. Weave in ends.

STITCH GUIDE

RIGHT-LEANING KNIT DECREASE Knit 2 together.

RIGHT-LEANING TWISTED KNIT DECREASE Slip 1 as if to purl. Remount the next stitch so it is rotated 180 degrees (one half turn) clockwise. Return the slipped stitch to the left needle. Knit 2 together.

RIGHT-LEANING PURL DECREASE Purl 2 together.

LEFT-LEANING KNIT DECREASE Slip 1 knitwise. Slip another 1 knitwise. Return slipped stitches to the left needle. Insert the right needle from the right to the left into the back loops of both stitches. Knit both together.

LEFT-LEANING TWISTED KNIT DECREASE Insert the right needle from the right to the left into the back loops of 2 stitches. Knit both together.

1 X 1 CABLE RIGHT TWISTED Slip 1 to cable needle, hold in back, knit 1 through the back loop, knit 1 through the back loop from cable needle.

1 X 1 CABLE LEFT TWISTED Slip 1 to cable needle, hold in front, knit 1 through the back loop, knit 1 through the back loop from cable needle.

LEFT CUFF CHART

4
3
2
1

20 19 18 17 16 15 14 13 12 11 10 9 8 7 6 5 4 3 2 1

LEFT MAIN CHART

24
23
22
21
20
19
18
17
16
15
14
13
12
11
10
9
8
7
6
5
4
3
2
1

20 19 18 17 16 15 14 13 12 11 10 9 8 7 6 5 4 3 2 1

	RS: Knit WS: Purl
	RS: Knit through the back loop WS: Purl through the back loop
	RS: Purl WS: Knit
→	Slip as if to purl
	Knit 1 through the back loop, yarn over, knit 1 through the back loop
	Knit 3 through the back loop
	Knit 1 through the back loop, drop 1 and unravel, knit 1 through the back loop
	1 x 1 Cable right twisted
	1 x 1 Cable left twisted
	Work these stitches 3 [4, 5, 6, 7] times

LEFT HEEL CHART

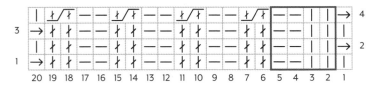

3
1

20 19 18 17 16 15 14 13 12 11 10 9 8 7 6 5 4 3 2 1

68

RIGHT CUFF CHART

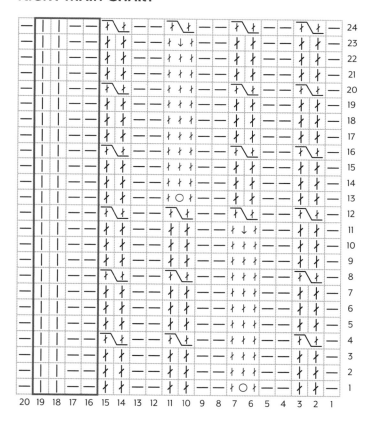

RIGHT MAIN CHART

RIGHT HEEL CHART

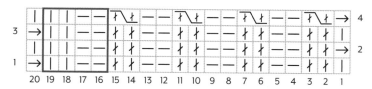

Distinct Moral Support

For traveling nothing is better than a costume of serge or other serviceable woollen goods, tailor-made. The hat should be chosen with discretion. A becoming one gives a woman a distinct moral support. It should be small, that the brim may not catch in the wind, and without feathers that fear dampness or flowers that fade in the sunshine.

Etiquette for All Occasions
Mrs. Burton Kingsland, 1901

Words cannot convey how much I adore the idea of a hat so becoming it provides moral support. This hat is so adorable it just might do the trick! The gathers on the side are created by working a short-row panel then using a tab to pull the brim up and crumple the extra fabric into lovely pleats. The result is delightfully asymmetric and totally flattering.

SHOWN IN Crème by Phydeaux in Seaglass. This is a DK-weight, 40% merino, 40% alpaca, 20% silk single-ply yarn.

GAUGE AND SIZING 21 stitches in 4 inches in stockinette. Fits a head of 18.5 [20, 21.75, 23.5] inches.

YARDAGE Shown with a 104-stitch cast on which used about 150 yards of yarn. You can probably make any size with 200 yards or less. You'll may want a decorative button.

NOTES

Use whatever needles give you the right gauge. That's *probably* something between a 3 and a 5, but you must swatch to be sure.

The rows surrounded by the heavy red border are repeated to make the tab as tall as you'd like. I recommend making it about 2 inches long.

WRAP AND TURN

With the yarn held to the inside of the hat, slip the next stitch to your right needle, bring the yarn to the outside of the hat, slip the same stitch back to your left needle. Now, turn your work so the other side of the material is facing you.

CAST ON Cast on 88 [96, 104, 112] stitches. Place marker and join for working in the round.

BRIM Knit the Brim Chart once.

SET UP ROUND Knit 25 [27, 29, 31] stitches. Thread a piece of scrap yarn on a needle and run it through the 6 stitches you just knit. Tie loosely to secure (leave the stitches on the needle, you're just marking out these stitches to make them easy to find later). Knit 19 [21, 23, 25] stitches. Place a middle of round marker (it should be exactly opposite your first marker). Knit to end of the round.

You have one marker at the start of the round, one at the middle, and 6 stitches between with a piece of scrap yarn run through them.

SHORT-ROW SECTION You will now work back and forth creating short rows to make the extra material for the ruched panel.

Row 1 (RS): K until 1 stitch remains before middle of the round marker. Wrap and turn.
Row 2 (WS): P until 1 stitch remains before the beginning of the round marker. Wrap and turn.
Row 3 (RS): K until 1 stitch remains before the last wrapped stitch. Wrap and turn.
Row 4 (WS): P until 1 stitch remains before the last wrapped stitch. Wrap and turn.

Work rows 3 and 4 15 [16, 17, 18] times.

Knit to end of round, removing middle of round marker as you pass it. When you come to the wrapped stitches, knit them, inserting the needle into the wrap first and then into the stitch. Knit 1 more round (again, when you come to the wrapped stitches, knit them, inserting the needle into the wrap first and then into the stitch).

BODY Knit every stitch of every round. Work until the hat reaches desired height before the decreases. The hat shown measures about 4 inches after the brim and before the decreases. Measure the height on the side opposite the short row panel.

DECREASES

Round 1: (Right-leaning k decrease, k9 [10, 11, 12]) 8 times.
Round 2: (Right-leaning k decrease, knit 1 stitch fewer than in the last round) 8 times.

Repeat round 2 until 8 stitches remain. Draw the yarn through remaining stitches.

TAB Locate the 6 stitches you marked with waste yarn. Slip them onto a needle and remove the waste yarn. Work the Tab Chart once, repeating the rows surrounded by the heavy red border until the tab is about 2 inches long. Break the yarn, leaving a fairly long tail (about a foot), and pass it through the final stitch. Pull the tab up until the point is about an inch above the top of your short-row section (allowing your short-row panel to crumple as you do) and use the tail to tack it in place.

FINISHING Weave in ends. Add a button if you like (it's just decorative, not functional). Block, adjusting the crumple on the short row panel while it's still damp so it will stay that way when it's dry. You can use safety pins to hold the crumples in place while the hat dries.

Brim Chart

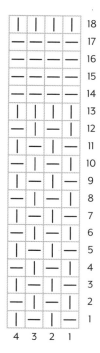

Tab Chart

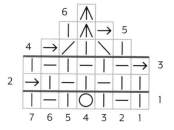

❘	RS: Knit WS: Purl
—	RS: Purl WS: Knit
→	Slip as if to purl
○	Yarn over
╱	WS: Right-leaning purl decrease
╲	WS: Left-leaning purl decrease
⋀	RS: Centered double knit decrease WS: Centered double purl decrease
▢	Repeat these 2 rows until tab reaches desired height (about 2 inches)

Stitch Guide

RIGHT-LEANING KNIT DECREASE Knit 2 together.

RIGHT-LEANING PURL DECREASE Purl 2 together.

LEFT-LEANING PURL DECREASE Slip 1 knitwise. Slip another 1 knitwise. Return slipped stitches to the left needle. Purl 2 together through the back loops.

CENTERED DOUBLE KNIT DECREASE Slip 2 together at the same time as if to knit 2 together. Knit 1. Pass the slipped stitches over.

CENTERED DOUBLE PURL DECREASE Slip 1 knitwise. Slip another 1 knitwise. Return these 2 stitches to the left needle in their new orientation. Swing your right needle around behind the fabric and insert it into these 2 stitches, from left to right, and slip them to your right needle. Purl 1. Pass the 2 slipped stitches, together as a set, over the stitch you just made.

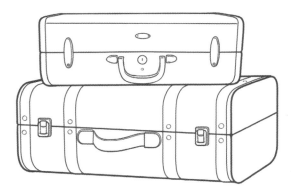

Women are Usually Obstinate

How common is the complaint among young women, especially those of sedentary habits, of chilliness, cold feet, and other symptoms of deficient circulation! And yet how impossible would it often be—for women are usually obstinate on this head—to induce them to exchange the thin silk stocking for a warm merino one!

The Ladies' Book of Etiquette and Manual of Politeness:
A Complete Hand Book for the use of the Lady in Polite Society
Florence Hartley, 1873

I have, on occasion, been known to be a bit obstinate. But I will gladly reach for warm merino socks when I'm feeling chilly. I suspect you will too especially if they are as pretty as these.

SHOWN IN Train Case by Mrs. Crosby in Boston Fern. This is a fingering-weight, 55% merino, 30% viscose, 15% nylon yarn with three plies.

GAUGE AND SIZING 9 stitches in 1 inch in stockinette. Fits a foot or leg of 7.25 [8, 9.75, 10.75] inches.

YARDAGE Shown with a 60-stitch cast on which used about 300 yards of yarn. You can probably make any size with 425 yards or less.

NOTES

Use whatever needles give you the right gauge. That's *probably* something between a 0 and a 2, but you must swatch to be sure.

The shaded stitches are used to adjust sizing. On all charts, work the unshaded stitches for the 60 & 80-stitch sizes. Work all stitches for 66 & 88-stitch sizes.

The stitches surrounded by the red border are repeated to adjust the size of the heel flap. Work them 1 [1, 2, 2] times.

CAST ON Cast on 60 [66, 80, 88] stitches. Place marker and join for working in the round.

CUFF Work the Cuff Chart once.

LEG Work the Main Chart until sock reaches desired height. Stop after completing row 4 of the Main Chart.

HEEL FLAP The heel flap is worked over stitches 32–60 [36–66, 42–80, 47–88]. It uses a total of 29 [31, 39, 42] stitches.

Row 1 is a wrong-side row. Row 2 is a right-side row. Work the Heel Chart 15 [16, 20, 21] times or until heel flap reaches desired length.

HEEL TURN Turn at the end of each row.

Row 1 (WS): Sl1, p15 [17, 21, 22], right-leaning p decrease, p1.
Row 2 (RS): Sl1, k4 [6, 6, 5], left-leaning k decrease, k1.
Row 3 (WS): Sl1, p5 [7, 7, 6], right-leaning p decrease, p1.
Row 4 (RS): Sl1, k6 [8, 8, 7], left-leaning k decrease, k1.
Row 5 (WS): Sl1, p7 [9, 9, 8], right-leaning p decrease, p1.
Row 6 (RS): Sl1, k8 [10, 10, 9], left-leaning k decrease, k1.
Row 7 (WS): Sl1, p9 [11, 11, 10], right-leaning p decrease, p1.
Row 8 (RS): Sl1, k10 [12, 12, 11], left-leaning k decrease, k1.
Row 9 (WS): Sl1, p11 [13, 13, 12], right-leaning p decrease, p1.
Row 10 (RS): Sl1, k12 [14, 14, 13], left-leaning k decrease, k1.
Row 11 (WS): Sl1, p13 [15, 15, 14], right-leaning p decrease, p1.
Row 12 (RS): Sl1, k14 [16, 16, 15], left-leaning k decrease, k1.

For 80 & 88-stitch sizes, as above plus:
Row 13 (WS): Sl1, p— [—, 17, 16], right-leaning p decrease, p1.
Row 14 (RS): Sl1, k— [—, 18, 17], left-leaning k decrease, k1.
Row 15 (WS): Sl1, p— [—, 19, 18], right-leaning p decrease, p1.
Row 16 (RS): Sl1, k— [—, 20, 19], left-leaning k decrease, k1.

For 88-stitch size, as above plus:
Row 17 (WS): Sl1, p— [—, —, 20], right-leaning p decrease, p1.
Row 18 (RS): Sl1, k— [—, —, 21], left-leaning k decrease, k1.

17 [19, 23, 24] stitches remain.

GUSSET AND FOOT

SETUP ROUND Pick up and knit stitches along the side of the heel flap, place first marker. Work across the top of the foot following the first row of the Main Chart (for the foot, you will always work 3 [3, 4, 4] full repeats of the Main Chart and 1 [2, 1, 2] additional purl stitches), place second marker. Pick up and knit stitches along the other side of the heel flap, k8 [9, 11, 12]. The round now begins in the middle of the bottom of the foot.

DECREASE ROUND Knit until 3 stitches remain before first marker, right-leaning k decrease, k1. Work across the top of the foot following the next row of the Main Chart. K1, left-leaning k decrease, knit to end of round. 2 stitches decreased.

NON-DECREASE ROUND Knit to first marker. Work across the top of the foot following the next row of the Main Chart. Knit to end of round.

Alternate decrease and non-decrease rounds until 62 [70, 82, 92] stitches remain. Repeat the non-decrease round until sock measures 1.75 [2, 2.5, 2.75] inches shorter than desired length. Stop after completing row 4 of the Main Chart.

TOE

DECREASE ROUND Knit until 3 stitches remain before first marker, right-leaning k decrease, k1. P1 [2, 1, 2], left-leaning k decrease, follow ribbing as established by row 5 of the Cuff Chart until 3 [4, 3, 4] stitches remain before second marker, right-leaning k decrease, p1 [2, 1, 2]. K1, left-leaning k decrease, knit to end of round. 4 stitches decreased.

NON-DECREASE ROUND Knit to first marker. Follow ribbing as established by row 5 of the Cuff Chart to second marker. Knit to end of round.

Work these 2 rounds 4 [6, 9, 11] times, 46 [46, 46, 48] stitches remain. Work the decrease round 5 more times, 26 [26, 26, 28] stitches remain. Knit to first marker. Remove markers. Graft toes. Weave in ends.

Cuff Chart

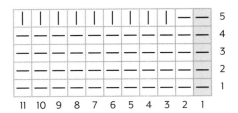

Main Chart

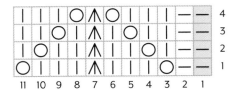

Heel Chart

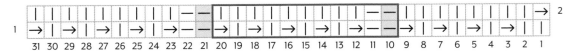

	RS: Knit WS: Purl
—	RS: Purl WS: Knit
→	Slip as if to purl
◯	Yarn over
⋀	Centered double knit decrease
☐	Work these stitches 1 [1, 2, 2] times
▨	Work for 66 & 88-stitch sizes

Stitch Guide

RIGHT-LEANING KNIT DECREASE Knit 2 together.

RIGHT-LEANING PURL DECREASE Purl 2 together.

LEFT-LEANING KNIT DECREASE Slip 1 knitwise. Slip another 1 knitwise. Return slipped stitches to the left needle. Insert the right needle from the right to the left into the back loops of both stitches. Knit both together.

CENTERED DOUBLE KNIT DECREASE Slip 2 together at the same time as if to knit 2 together. Knit 1. Pass the slipped stitches over.

In Case of Draughts

Young married women are allowed to be as magnificent as a picture of Marie de Medici, and can wear on New-Year's day rose-coloured and white brocaded silks with pearl trimmings, or plain ciel blue, or prawn-colored silk over white, or embossed velvet, or what they please…Each lady should have near her an ermine cloak, or a small camel's-hair shawl in case of draughts.

Manners and Social Usages
Mrs. John Sherwood, 1887

While this shawl will, of course, look lovely at whatever New Year's Day festivities you might happen to attend, I think you should reach for it year round. Chilly spring evenings, over-zealous air conditioners, and ocean breezes all offer their own drafts, and this shawl will happily fend them off and look lovely doing it.

SHOWN IN Oasis by Anzula in Seaside. This is a DK-weight, 70% silk, 30% camel yarn with two plies.

GAUGE AND SIZING 16 stitches in 4 inches in stockinette. Measures 14.75 [18.25, 21.75] inches in width, length adjustable.

YARDAGE Shown with a 59-stitch cast on and 72-inch length which used about 625 yards of yarn. A similar length can be made with about 800 yards with a 73-stitch cast on or 950 yards with an 87-stitch cast on.

NOTES

Use whatever needles give you the right gauge. That's *probably* something between a 4 and a 6, but you must swatch to be sure.

Odd rows are wrong-side rows. Even rows are right-side rows.

The stitches surrounded by the red border are repeated to adjust the size of the shawl. Work them 1 [2, 3] times.

CAST ON Cast on 59. [73, 87] stitches.

WEIGHING YOUR WORK I *strongly* suggest weighing your knitting at several points as you work. This will help you to know if you have enough yarn to work another repeat of the pattern or if it's time to get ready to finish the piece.

Weigh your project after you've worked 33 rows (and make a note of this weight). That's a generous estimate of how much yarn you'll need to work one more repeat of the Middle Chart.

Weigh your project after you've worked 52 rows (and make a note of this weight). That's a generous estimate of how much yarn you'll need to work the Final Chart and bind off.

Add those two weights together, and you'll know how much yarn you need to work one more repeat of the Middle Chart and still be able to work the Final Chart.

Keep in mind that your yarn usage may vary slightly over the course of your project. Because of this, it's always a good idea to round *up* when weighing your knitting (if your scale says 12.4 grams, round up to 13 grams) and round *down* when weighing your remaining yarn (if your scale says 24.8 grams round down to 24 grams).

BODY Work the Initial Chart once. Work the Middle Chart until the shawl is about 8 inches shorter than desired length. Stop after completing row 32 of the Middle Chart. Work the Final Chart once.

FINISHING Bind off loosely. Weave in ends. Block vigorously, pulling the points out to emphasize them.

Initial Chart

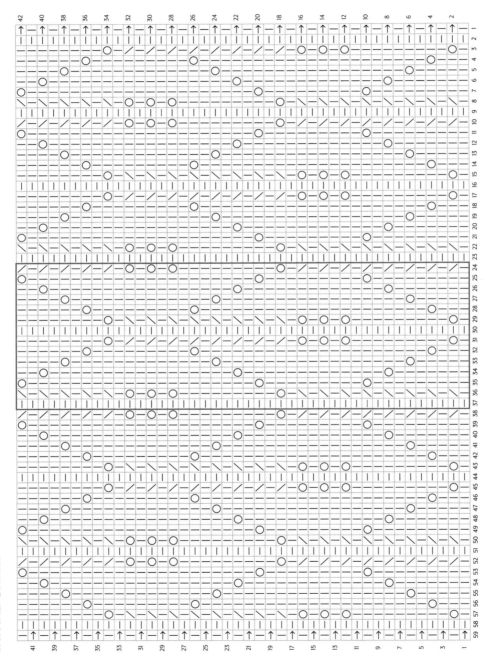

	RS: Knit WS: Purl
—	RS: Purl WS: Knit
→	Slip as if to purl
◯	Yarn over
╱	Right-leaning knit decrease
╲	Left-leaning knit decrease
☐	Work these stitches 1 [2, 3] times

STITCH GUIDE

RIGHT-LEANING KNIT DECREASE: Knit 2 together.

LEFT-LEANING KNIT DECREASE Slip 1 knitwise. Slip another 1 knitwise. Return slipped stitches to the left needle. Insert the right needle from the right to the left into the back loops of both stitches. Knit both together.

MIDDLE CHART

FINAL CHART

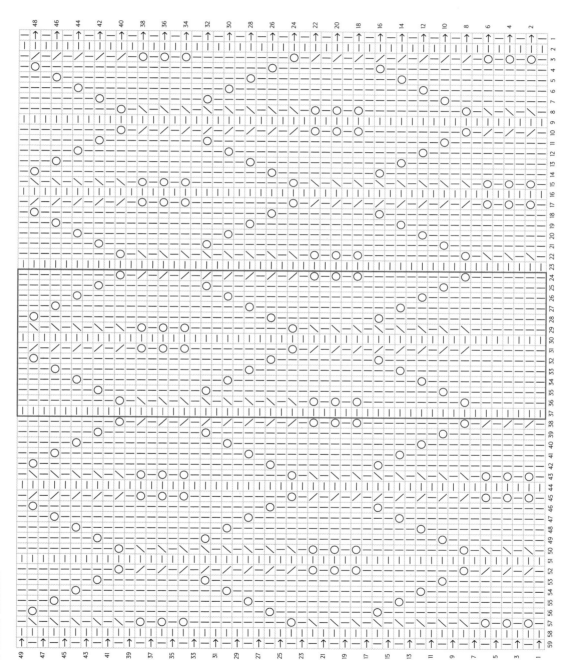

Which has Moved the Poet

It seems hardly necessary to say to an American lady that she should be neatly dressed at breakfast…The hair should be carefully arranged, and the feet…in the natty stocking and well-fitting slipper, which has moved the poet to such feeling verses.

Good Manners for All Occasions:
Including Etiquette of Cards, Wedding Announcements and Invitations
Margaret E Sangster, 1904

I can't quite promise that these socks will cause poets to spring up out of the ether and compose odes to your charming feet, but I wouldn't exactly rule it out either. If it should happen, do get in touch. I definitely want to hear about it.

SHOWN IN Socks that Rock Medium-weight by Blue Moon Fiber Arts in Mermaid Tears. This is a sport-weight, 100% superwash merino yarn with three plies.

GAUGE AND SIZING 8 stitches in 1 inch in stockinette. Fits a foot or leg of 6.5 [8.25, 9.75, 11.25] inches.

YARDAGE Shown with a 60-stitch cast on which used about 300 yards of yarn. You can probably make any size with 400 yards or less.

NOTES

Use whatever needles give you the right gauge. That's *probably* something between a 0 and a 2, but you must swatch to be sure.

The stitches surrounded by the red border are repeated to adjust the size of the heel flap. Work them 2 [3, 4, 5] times.

To make the socks mirror each other, for the 60 & 84-stitch sizes, start following the Main Chart on row 1 for the first sock and on row 9 for the second sock.

CAST ON Cast on 48 [60, 72, 84] stitches. Place marker and join for working in the round.

LEG Work the Main Chart until sock reaches desired height. Stop after completing row 8 or row 16 of the Main Chart. To make the socks mirror each other, for the 60 & 84-stitch sizes, start following the Main Chart on row 1 for the first sock and on row 9 for the second sock

HEEL FLAP The heel flap is worked over stitches 26–48 [32–60, 38–72, 44–84]. It uses a total of 23 [29, 35, 41] stitches.

Row 1 is a wrong-side row. Row 2 is a right-side row. Work the Heel Chart 12 [15, 18, 21] times or until heel flap reaches desired length.

HEEL TURN Turn at the end of each row.

Row 1 (WS): Sl1, p13 [15, 19, 21], right-leaning p decrease, p1.
Row 2 (RS): Sl1, k6 [4, 6, 4], left-leaning k decrease, k1.
Row 3 (WS): Sl1, p7 [5, 7, 5], right-leaning p decrease, p1.
Row 4 (RS): Sl1, k8 [6, 8, 6], left-leaning k decrease, k1.
Row 5 (WS): Sl1, p9 [7, 9, 7], right-leaning p decrease, p1.
Row 6 (RS): Sl1, k10 [8, 10, 8], left-leaning k decrease, k1.
Row 7 (WS): Sl1, p11 [9, 11, 9], right-leaning p decrease, p1.
Row 8 (RS): Sl1, k12 [10, 12, 10], left-leaning k decrease, k1.

For 60, 72, & 84-stitch sizes, as above plus:
Row 9 (WS): Sl1, p— [11, 13, 11], right-leaning p decrease, p1.
Row 10 (RS): Sl1, k— [12, 14, 12], left-leaning k decrease, k1.
Row 11 (WS): Sl1, p— [13, 15, 13], right-leaning p decrease, p1.
Row 12 (RS): Sl1, k— [14, 16, 14], left-leaning k decrease, k1.

For 72 & 84-stitch sizes, as above plus:
Row 13 (WS): Sl1, p— [—, 17, 15], right-leaning p decrease, p1.
Row 14 (RS): Sl1, k— [—, 18, 16], left-leaning k decrease, k1.

For 84-stitch size, as above plus:
Row 15 (WS): Sl1, p— [—, —, 17], right-leaning p decrease, p1.
Row 16 (RS): Sl1, k— [—, —, 18], left-leaning k decrease, k1.
Row 17 (WS): Sl1, p— [—, —, 19], right-leaning p decrease, p1.
Row 18 (RS): Sl1, k— [—, —, 20], left-leaning k decrease, k1.

15 [17, 21, 23] stitches remain.

GUSSET AND FOOT

SETUP ROUND Pick up and knit stitches along the side of the heel flap, place first marker. Work across the top of the foot following the

next row of the Main Chart (for the foot, you will always work 2 [2, 3, 3] full repeats of the Main Chart and 1 [7, 1, 7] stitches from an additional repeat), place second marker. Pick up and knit stitches along the other side of the heel flap, k8 [9, 10, 11]. The round now begins in the middle of the bottom of the foot.

DECREASE ROUND Knit until 3 stitches remain before first marker, right-leaning k decrease, k1. Work across the top of the foot following the next row of the Main Chart. K1, left-leaning k decrease, knit to end of round. 2 stitches decreased.

NON-DECREASE ROUND Knit to first marker. Work across the top of the foot following the next row of the Main Chart. Knit to end of round.

Alternate decrease and non-decrease rounds until 50 [62, 74, 86] stitches remain. Repeat the non-decrease round until sock measures 1.25 [1.75, 2.5, 3] inches shorter than desired length. Stop after completing row 8 or 16 of the Main Chart. Repeat row 1 of the Main Chart as needed to adjust length.

TOE

DECREASE ROUND Knit until 3 stitches remain before first marker, right-leaning k decrease, k1. P1, left-leaning k decrease, follow ribbing as established by row 1 of the Main Chart until 3 stitches remain before second marker, right-leaning k decrease, p1. K1, left-leaning k decrease, knit to end of round. 4 stitches decreased.

NON-DECREASE ROUND Knit to first marker. Follow ribbing as established by row 1 of the Main Chart to second marker. Knit to end of round.

Work these 2 rounds 2 [5, 8, 11] times, 42 stitches remain. Work the decrease round 5 more times, 22 stitches remain. Knit to first marker. Remove markers. Graft toes. Weave in ends.

MAIN CHART

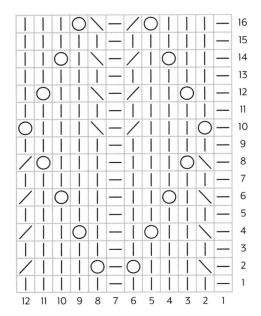

STITCH GUIDE

RIGHT-LEANING KNIT DECREASE Knit 2 together.

RIGHT-LEANING PURL DECREASE Purl 2 together.

LEFT-LEANING KNIT DECREASE Slip 1 knitwise. Slip another 1 knitwise. Return slipped stitches to the left needle. Insert the right needle from the right to the left into the back loops of both stitches. Knit both together.

HEEL CHART

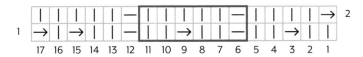

	RS: Knit WS: Purl
—	RS: Purl WS: Knit
→	Slip as if to purl
O	Yarn over
/	Right-leaning knit decrease
\	Left-leaning knit decrease
	Work these stitches 2 [3, 4,5] times

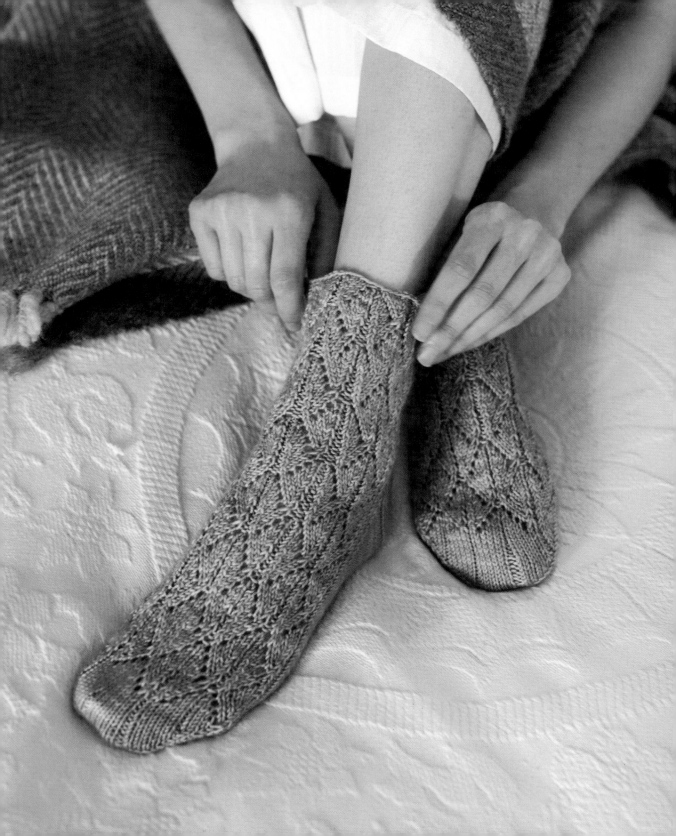

Perfectly Finished in Every Point

Be careful always that the details of your dress are perfectly finished in every point. The small articles of a wardrobe require constant care to keep in perfect order, yet they will wofully revenge themselves if neglected. Let the collar, handkerchief, boots, gloves, and belts be always whole, neat, and adapted to the dress.

The Ladies' Book of Etiquette and Manual of Politeness:
A Complete Hand Book for the use of the Lady in Polite Society
Florence Hartley, 1860

I'm not going to manage "constant care" for all my accessories. And if my handkerchiefs want to plot revenge as a result of my neglect? Well, I think I'm up for the challenge. But these cuffs might just be cute enough to warrant a bit of extra attention. They are worked flat and buttoned around your wrist. You can make them short and wear them as cuffs or make them long, leave a few buttons unbuttoned to create a thumb hole, and wear them as fingerless mitts.

SHOWN IN Civility Fingering by Elemental Affects in Limoncella. This is a sport-weight, 70% merino, 30% silk yarn with three plies.

GAUGE AND SIZING 7 stitches in 1 inch in stockinette. Fits a wrist of 5.75 [6.5, 7.5, 8.25] inches.

YARDAGE Shown with a 54-stitch cast on which used about 75 (shorter cuff) to 100 (longer mitt) yards of yarn. You can probably make any size with 125 yards or less. You'll also want a handful of small shank buttons.

NOTES

Use whatever needles give you the right gauge. That's *probably* something between a 2 and a 4, but you must swatch to be sure.

Odd rows are wrong-side rows. Even rows are right-side rows.

The stitches surrounded by the red border are repeated to adjust the size of the cuff. Work them 6 [7, 8, 9] times.

The rows surrounded by the gray border are repeated to make the cuff longer.

CAST ON Cast on 48 [54, 60, 66] stitches.

CUFF The cuff is worked flat and buttoned around your wrist.

To make the right and left cuff match, you need to pay a bit of attention to the buttonholes.

When you're working the left mitt, only work the buttonholes on the left side of the chart (columns 16 and 17). Ignore the buttonholes on the right side of the chart (columns 3 and 4) and just pretend the chart shows purl stitches there instead (and, since that's a wrong side row, you'll actually make a knit stitch as you're working).

When you're working the right mitt, only work the buttonholes on the right side of the chart (columns 3 and 4). Ignore the buttonholes on the left side of the chart (columns 16 and 17) and just pretend the chart shows purl stitches there instead (and, since that's a wrong side row, you'll actually make a knit stitch as you're working).

Work rows 1–4 of the Main Chart once. Work rows 5–14 of the Main Chart until cuff is about half an inch shorter than desired length. Work rows 15–19 of the Main Chart once.

FINISHING Weave in ends. Attach buttons opposite buttonholes. Block, emphasizing the point at the middle of the piece.

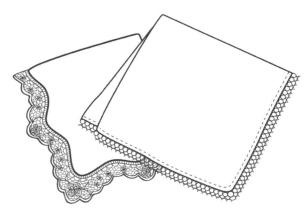

MAIN CHART

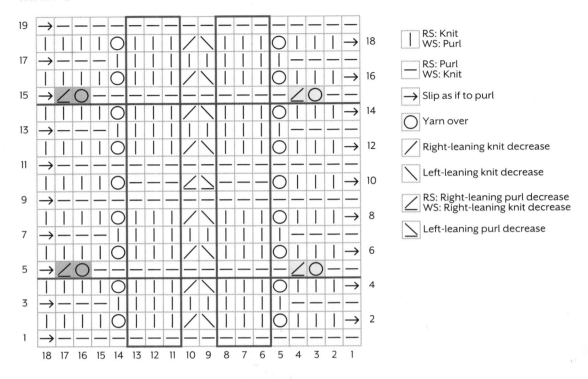

RS: Knit
WS: Purl

RS: Purl
WS: Knit

→ Slip as if to purl

○ Yarn over

╱ Right-leaning knit decrease

╲ Left-leaning knit decrease

RS: Right-leaning purl decrease
WS: Right-leaning knit decrease

Left-leaning purl decrease

STITCH GUIDE

RIGHT-LEANING KNIT DECREASE Knit 2 together.

RIGHT-LEANING PURL DECREASE Purl 2 together.

LEFT-LEANING KNIT DECREASE Slip 1 knitwise. Slip another 1 knitwise. Return slipped stitches to the left needle. Insert the right needle from the right to the left into the back loops of both stitches. Knit both together.

LEFT-LEANING PURL DECREASE Slip 1 knitwise. Slip another 1 knitwise. Return slipped stitches to the left needle. Purl 2 together through the back loops.

Work these stitches 6 [7, 8, 9] times

Work these rows until cuff reaches desired height

These are the button holes for the right cuff. Work them only when making the right cuff. When making the left cuff, pretend the chart shows a purl stitch here.

These are the button holes for the left cuff. Work them only when making the left cuff. When making the right cuff, pretend the chart shows a purl stitch here.

Faultlessly Neat

A true gentlewoman is always faultlessly neat. No richness of toilette in the afternoon, no diamonds in the evening, can atone for unbrushed hair, a soiled collar, or untidy slippers at breakfast.

Routledge's Manual of Etiquette
George Routledge and Sons, between 1858 & 1882

Asking anyone to tend to their hair before they've had a restorative cup of coffee or tea sounds like a bit too much to hope for. Let's just focus on the slippers. I'm pretty sure these are cute enough that they will distract from anything your hair might get up to first thing in the morning.

SHOWN IN Pediboo Sport Tonals by Frog Tree in 1464. This is a sport-weight, 80% merino, 20% bamboo yarn with three plies.

GAUGE AND SIZING 6.5 stitches in 1 inch in stockinette. Fits a foot of 7.5 [8.25, 8.75, 9.5, 10.25] inches (measure around the widest part of the ball of the foot).

YARDAGE Shown with a 27-stitch cast on which used about 150 yards of yarn. You can probably make any size with 225 yards or less.

NOTES

Use whatever needles give you the right gauge. That's *probably* something between a 2 and a 4, but you must swatch to be sure.

The first portion of the slipper is knit flat, the second portion is worked in the round. But the portion that is worked flat is rather U-shaped, and so you will almost certainly want to work on DPNs or circular needles to make your knitting easier. You'll also need spare DPNs of the same size or slightly smaller a bit later in the process.

The stitches surrounded by the red border are repeated to adjust sizing. Work them 29 [33, 27, 41, 45] times.

CAST ON Cast on 27 [27, 31, 31, 35] stitches.

HEEL FLAP Turn at the end of each row.

Row 1 (WS): Sl1, (p1 through the back loop, k1) 12 [12, 14, 14, 16] times, p1 through the back loop, p1.
Row 2 (RS): Sl1, (k1 through the back loop, p1) 12 [12, 14, 14, 16] times, k1 through the back loop, k1.

Work these 2 rows 18 [20, 21, 23, 24] times.

HEEL TURN Turn at the end of each row.

Row 1 (WS): Sl1, p15 [15, 17, 17, 19], right-leaning p decrease, p1.
Row 2 (RS): Sl1, k6 [6, 6, 6, 6], left-leaning k decrease, k1.
Row 3 (WS): Sl1, p7 [7, 7, 7, 7], right-leaning p decrease, p1.
Row 4 (RS): Sl1, k8 [8, 8, 8, 8], left-leaning k decrease, k1.
Row 5 (WS): Sl1, p9 [9, 9, 9, 9], right-leaning p decrease, p1.
Row 6 (RS): Sl1, k10 [10, 10, 10, 10], left-leaning k decrease, k1.
Row 7 (WS): Sl1, p11 [11, 11, 11, 11], right-leaning p decrease, p1.
Row 8 (RS): Sl1, k12 [12, 12, 12, 12], left-leaning k decrease, k1.
Row 9 (WS): Sl1, p13 [13, 13, 13, 13], right-leaning p decrease, p1.
Row 10 (RS): Sl1, k14 [14, 14, 14, 14], left-leaning k decrease, k1.

For 31, 31, & 35-stitch sizes, as above plus:
Row 11 (WS): Sl1, p— [—, 15, 15, 15], right-leaning p decrease, p1.
Row 12 (RS): Sl1, k— [—, 16, 16, 16], left-leaning k decrease, k1.

For 35-stitch size, as above plus:
Row 13 (WS): Sl1, p— [—, —, —, 17], right-leaning p decrease, p1.
Row 14 (RS): Sl1, k— [—, —, —, 18], left-leaning k decrease, k1.

17 [17, 19, 19, 21] stitches remain.

Final row (WS): Sl1, purl to end of row.

Break the yarn, leaving a tail to weave in later.

SET UP ROW Hold the heel flap in front of you with the outside of the heel flap facing you and the heel turn at the bottom. While holding the heel flap in this position, locate the top left-hand corner of the heel flap.

With a new piece of yarn, starting at this corner, pick up and knit 19 [21, 22, 24, 25] stitches along the side of the heel flap. Knit across the 17 [17, 19, 19, 21] stitches of the sole. Pick up and knit 19 [21, 22, 24, 25] stitches along the side of the heel flap. You will have 55 [59, 63, 67, 71] stitches on your needles.

Begin following the Main Chart. Odd rows are wrong-side rows. Even rows are right-side rows.

Work the Main Chart until you'd like to have the sides of your slipper meet. I recommend working it until you are at or very near the ball of your foot (when in doubt, stop sooner rather than later). Stop after completing row 20 of the Main Chart. Break the yarn, leaving a tail to weave in later.

JOIN FOR WORKING IN THE ROUND Take a moment to examine your knitting. You have a heel flap and a U-shaped section of knitting that wraps around your foot. If you slip your foot into your knitting, you'll have a cable panel on the left side of your foot, a plain stockinette sole under your foot, and a cable panel on the right side of your foot. Those cable panels are each 13 stitches wide.

To join your knitting for working in the round, first place the 13 stitches of each of these cabled panels on it's own DPN. Now bring one of the panels over the other. For the left slipper, bring the left panel over the right panel. For the right slipper, bring the right panel over the left panel.

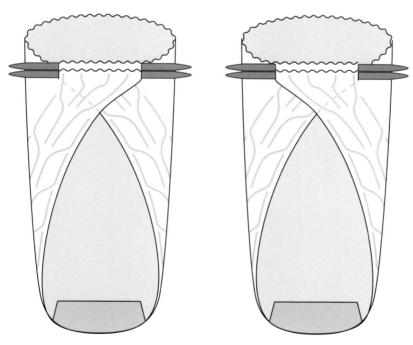

LEFT SLIPPER The left panel goes on top.

RIGHT SLIPPER The right panel goes on top.

Once the panels are arranged, work the stitches of the panels together. Do this by working across row 1 of the Foot Chart (being sure you're going into first the rightmost stitch on the upper and then rightmost stitch on the lower DPN as you do). In other words, each stitch of the row will join together a stitch from the top DPN and a stitch from the bottom DPN. This will both join your knitting up into a circle and decrease the number of stitches on your needles by 13.

Once you've worked across all 13 stitches in this fashion, you'll have 42 [46, 50, 54, 58] stitches on your needles.

Knit 4 [5, 6, 7, 8] more stitches. Place a marker (called second marker). Knit 21 [23, 25, 27, 29] stitches. Place another marker (called first marker, the round now begins at this marker). The markers separate the top and bottom of the slipper.

Take a moment to check that you've got the same number of stitches between markers (you should have 21 [23, 25, 27, 29] stitches on the top and the same number on the bottom). Also check that the cabled panel is evenly spaced between the markers (you should have 4 [5, 6, 7, 8] knit stitches between the markers and the edges of the panel.

NORMAL ROUND K4 [5, 6, 7, 8], work across the next row of the Foot Chart, Knit to end of round.

Work normal round until slipper measures 1.5 [1.75, 1.75, 2, 2] inches shorter than desired length. Stop after completing row 1, 2, 3, 4, 5, or 13 of the Foot Chart. Repeat row 1 of the Foot Chart as needed to adjust length.

TOE

DECREASE ROUND K1, left-leaning k decrease, work in pattern as established by row 1 of the Foot Chart until 3 stitches remain before second marker, right-leaning k decrease, k1. K1, left-leaning k decrease, knit until 3 stitches remain before first marker, right-leaning k decrease, k1. 4 stitches decreased.

Work this round 7 [8, 9, 10, 11] times. 14 stitches remain. Remove markers. Graft toes. Weave in ends.

Main Chart

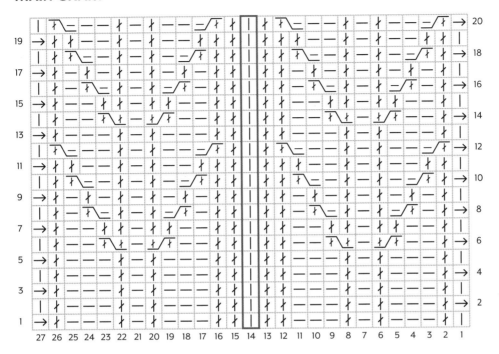

RS: Knit / WS: Purl

	RS: Knit / WS: Purl
	RS: Knit through the back loop / WS: Purl through the back loop
	RS: Purl / WS: Knit
→	Slip as if to purl
⸝/⸝	1 x 1 Cable right twisted
⸜\⸜	1 x 1 Cable left twisted
—/⸝	1 x 1 Cable right twisted over purl
⸜\—	1 x 1 Cable left twisted over purl
	Work this stitch 29 [33, 37, 41, 45] times

Foot Chart

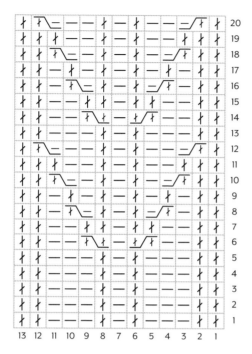

Stitch Guide

RIGHT-LEANING KNIT DECREASE Knit 2 together.

RIGHT-LEANING PURL DECREASE Purl 2 together.

LEFT-LEANING KNIT DECREASE Slip 1 knitwise. Slip another 1 knitwise. Return slipped stitches to the left needle. Insert the right needle from the right to the left into the back loops of both stitches. Knit both together.

1 X 1 CABLE RIGHT TWISTED Slip 1 to cable needle, hold in back, knit 1 through the back loop, knit 1 through the back loop from cable needle.

1 X 1 CABLE LEFT TWISTED Slip 1 to cable needle, hold in front, knit 1 through the back loop, knit 1 through the back loop from cable needle.

1 X 1 CABLE RIGHT TWIST OVER PURL Slip 1 to cable needle, hold in back, knit 1 through the back loop, purl 1 from cable needle.

1 X 1 CABLE LEFT TWIST OVER PURL Slip 1 to cable needle, hold in front, purl 1, knit 1 through the back loop from cable needle.

Suggestions

ABBREVIATIONS I've kept abbreviations to a bare minimum. K for knit, P for purl, SL for slip, RS for right side, and WS for wrong side. Everything else is written out.

BLOCKING Knitting almost always looks better once it's been blocked. You've spent hours knitting—it's worth it to spend a few extra minutes blocking to really show off your work!

Start by soaking your project in cool water (perhaps with a bit of your favorite wool wash) for at least half an hour. Then, remove it from the water, roll it up an a towel, and gently squeeze out excess water. The next step is to shape your knitting. How you shape it depends on the project.

Some things don't require much persuasion. Socks just need to be patted and smoothed into shape (if you have sock blockers, it's even easier). Hats can be set over an appropriately sized bowl (wrap a hand towel around the bowl first if it's not quite big enough). And I've had fabulous luck blocking fingerless mitts on shampoo bottles.

Others projects, shawls in particular, benefit from a more aggressive treatment. You'll want to break out the pins, yard stick, and blocking mats (use a spare bed if you don't have mats). Don't be afraid to tug hard and really open up the fabric. Lace behaves better if you're a bit bossy with it. This is also the moment to really emphasize any points or waves on the edges of your shawl. Tug them out and pin them in place.

Then, just wait for everything to dry. I know it's hard, but all your blocking will have been in vain if you don't let it dry all the way.

BORDERS Some charts use heavy borders to draw your attention to certain stitches. These stitches are generally worked more than once to adjust the size of the project. When this happens, there will be a note explaining the specific instructions for that particular pattern. Please be sure to read these notes carefully before you begin.

CAST ON Use any stretchy cast on you like. The projects here used the long-tailed cast on unless they say otherwise.

CAST OFF Use any stretchy cast off you like.

CHARTS All the patterns use at least one chart. Charts are easy to follow, but they do require a bit of attention if you've not used them before. The important thing to remember is that charts show you a stylized picture of what the right side of your knitting looks like.

If you're working in the round, the right side of your fabric is always facing you, so the chart always shows you exactly what to do.

113

Just read each row of the chart from right to left and make the stitch indicated in the stitch key.

If you're working flat, the procedure is a bit different. When you're working a right-side row, read that row of the chart from right to left and make the stitch indicated in the right-side (RS) instructions in the stitch key. When you're working a wrong-side row, read that row of the chart from left to right and make the stitch indicated in the wrong-side (WS) instructions in the stitch key.

The pattern will tell you if a particular chart starts with a right-side or wrong-side row, but you can also tell from the chart. If you're working a right-side row, the row number will be on the right of the chart. If you're working a wrong-side row, the row number will be on the left of the chart.

Whether you're working in the round or flat, you always start at the bottom of the chart and work your way up, one row at a time.

GAUGE Always knit a gauge swatch (in the stitch specified) to check your gauge. I promise it saves both time and heartbreak in the end.

GRAFTING Graft your toes however you like. The projects here used Kitchener stitch.

HEEL FLAPS Heel flaps are worked back and forth over about half the stitches of the sock. Each sock pattern lists the specific stitches that are to be used for the heel flap. Be sure to read carefully to see which stitches to use.

It is easy to adjust the height of your heel flap to make your sock really fit your foot. Just be sure to work an even number of rows so you're lined up properly to continue with the heel turn.

NEEDLES Use whatever style of needles you prefer (DPNs or circular needles for knitting in the round; straights, DPNs or circulars for knitting flat).

The needle size ranges are *only suggestions*. You should use whatever needle size you need to get the right gauge. Matching gauge is way more important than either using the needle size listed in the pattern or the needle size given on the ball band of your yarn.

NOTES Each pattern includes notes in a column to the side of the pattern. They're important. This is where things like shaded stitches, stitches surrounded by a border, and how to make your socks mirror each other are explained. Do yourself a favor and read the notes carefully before you begin.

PATTERN REPEATS Generally, a chart shows one full repeat of a stitch pattern. Unless otherwise noted, this stitch pattern is worked across the entire row or round of the piece. Put another way, "work the chart" means repeat the stitches of the chart over and over across the entire row or round until you reach the end of the row or round.

RIGHT SIDE The right side of your knitting is the outside or the public side. It is abbreviated RS.

SHADED STITCHES Some charts use shading to draw your attention to certain stitches. This is generally done to adjust the size of a project. When this happens, there will be a note explaining exactly what's going on. Please be sure to read these notes carefully before you begin.

SIZING Each pattern is offered in several sizes. Stitch counts, pattern repeats, or other instructions generally differ from size to size.

This is indicated by first giving the information for the smallest size then giving it for the larger sizes in square brackets. If there is more than one larger size, the information for larger sizes will be separated by commas. So the instruction "Cast on 24 [36, 48] stitches" means cast on 24 stitches for the smallest size, cast on 36 stitches for the medium size, or cast on 48 stitches for the largest size.

SLIPPED STITCHES Always slip as if to purl with the yarn to the private side of the work unless told otherwise.

Many of the projects call for slipping stitches along the edge of the knitting to create a tidy selvage edge. There are almost as many ways to do this as there are knitters. If you're getting uniform, elongated stitches along the edges of the fabric, you're doing it right! If you have a method you like, stick with it.

If you're having a hard time with it, one approach that works for many people is to always slip the first stitch as if to purl with your yarn held to the wrong side of the fabric. If you find that's not working for the way you knit, you can also try holding the yarn to the back of the work and slipping as if to knit on right-side rows and holding the yarn to the front of the work and slipping as if to purl on wrong-side rows.

STITCH GUIDES Any unusual stitches are defined in the pattern. Look for the Stitch Guide in each pattern for details.

STITCH MARKERS Many patterns suggest using a stitch marker to indicate the beginning of the round or other points of note. If you prefer, you can usually arrange your needles to indicate this instead.

TOES Several of the socks have a bit of patterning on the toes. If you find that bothers your toes, you can always substitute stockinette instead.

It is easy to adjust the shape of the toes to fit your feet. Most of the socks here have you decrease every other row until about half of your decreases are done and then decrease every round. If you've got pointy toes, you may want to decrease every other round until closer to three quarters of your decreases are done. If you've got flat toes, you may want to decrease every other round until only one quarter of your decreases are done.

WRONG SIDE The wrong side of your knitting is the inside or the private side. It is abbreviated WS.

YARN REQUIREMENTS Each pattern lists the approximate yardage used for the project shown and suggests the maximum you might need to make any size.

This is a good guideline, but estimating yardage requirements is a bit of a black art. If you decide to make the leg of your sock 10 inches tall or to make your fingerless gloves elbow length, you'll need more yarn. When in doubt, buy extra! It's easier to return an unneeded skein than to run out on the last row.

Resources

A Lady is Known Carnal by Vice in Concrete.
VICEYARNS.COM

By Naughty Design Lush Twist by The Uncommon Thread in Tea Smoked .
THEUNCOMMONTHREAD.CO.UK

Distinct Moral Support Crème by Phydeaux Designs in Seaglass.
PHYDEAUX-DESIGNS.COM

Essential to Perfection Finch by Quince & Co in Iceland.
QUINCEANDCO.COM

Faultlessly Neat Pediboo Sport Tonal by Frogtree in 1464.
FROGTREEYARNS.COM

General Country Sports Ghillie Sport by Bare Naked Wools in Cream.
BARENAKEDWOOLS.COM

In Case of Draughts Oasis by Anzula in Seaside.
ANZULA.COM

Just Which Is In Vogue Lust by Alchemy: Yarns of Transformation in Amethyst.
ALCHEMYYARNS.COM

Knowledge of What Was Sensible Staccato by Shibui in Caffeine.
SHIBUIKNITS.COM

Perfectly Finished in Every Point Civility Fingering by Elemental Affects in Limoncella.
ELEMENTALAFFECTS.COM

Singularly Disenchanting Shepherd Sock by Lorna's Laces in Buckingham Fountain.
LORNASLACES.NET

Suitable for Use Trinity Worsted by SweetGeorgia in Silver.
SWEETGEORGIAYARNS.COM

Treacherous Winds Fino by Manos Del Uruguay in Rosewater.
MANOSYARNS.COM

Which has Moved The Poet Socks That Rock Mediumweight by Blue Moon Fiber Arts in Mermaid Tears.
BLUEMOONFIBERARTS.COM

Women are Usually Obstinate Train Case by Mrs. Crosby in Boston Fern.
MRSCROSBYPLAYS.COM

Charts created with Stitchmastery.
STITCHMASTERY.COM

Photos by Zoë Lonergan.
ZOELONERGAN.COM

Acknowledgements

I'll let you in on a little secret. The first book is the hard one. If you make it through the first book, you will have built a team. And your team will get you through the next book. I've been doing this long enough that I have a heck of a team, and I wouldn't dream of doing it without them.

I must start by offering my thanks to the intrepid sample knitters who take my scattershot first drafts and turn them into the lovely knitted objects you see in these pages. Katie Metzroth, Heather Robinson, Rhonda Wilson, and Laura Lazarites all worked tirelessly to create these pieces, and I am in their debt.

But knitting is only part of the process; you need pictures, too. Brian Glenn, Laura Lazarites, Lauren Miller, and Stacy Siddle spent a very gray, very wet April day with me making sure we had exactly what we needed. Zoë Lonergan took beautiful pictures (and kept me from having a complete fit when the rain threatened to spoil our fun). And Five Oaks, the home of the Massillon Woman's Club, provided the perfect backdrop.

As important as knitting and pictures are, the book wouldn't be much good without a few words here and there. That's where Cathy Scott and Heather Ordover come in. Cathy not only made the amazing program, StitchMastery, with which I drew the charts but also edited my patterns. And Heather, between episodes of her marvelous CraftLit podcast, found time to edit the rest of the book. If you made it through the book without cursing my name, it's thanks to their hard work (and if you are hurling curses at me, it's almost certainly because I foolishly ignored their good advice).

The alarmingly talented Lana Holden and Anna Kuo made this book ever so much more fun to use. Lana created the marvelous schematics, and Anna drew the wonderful illustrations scattered throughout the text.

Members of Cat Bordhi's Visionary Authors group were among the first to hear about my plans for this book, and they have offered unwavering encouragement and enthusiasm throughout its creation.

And of course, many thanks to my family for their support of this odd thing I do, especially to my husband Brian. Since I started this adventure, he's stacked countless boxes of books, bent websites to my will, cheerfully modeled an alarming number of socks, and spent far more time reading knitting books than any non-knitter should. I couldn't do it without him.

Other Works

Curls: Versatile, Wearable Wraps to Knit at Any Gauge

The Knitter's Curiosity Cabinet Volume I: 20 Patterns Inspired by Vintage Botanical Illustrations

The Knitter's Curiosity Cabinet Volume II: 18 Patterns Inspired by Vintage Butterfly Illustrations

The Knitter's Curiosity Cabinet Volume III: 18 Patterns Inspired by Vintage Marine Illustrations